Can U Love Me

A Memoir…A Tribute

Can U Love Me

A Memoir…A Tribute

Nicholas "*NinosCorner*" Battle

Foreword by: Langston Collin Wilkins, PhD

and

Jerome "*SoundsGoodAlready*" Stampley

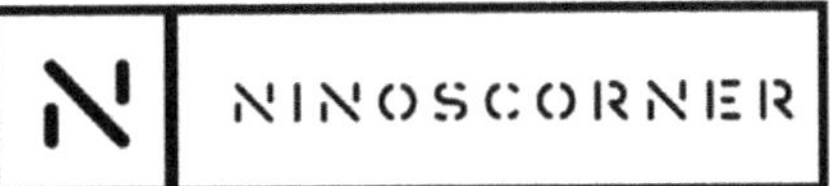

2019

Dedication

This book is dedicated to my son LanLan. You will never understand how much you have changed my life. You truly inspired me to start writing and without you, this book would have never come to fruition. To my wife, my rock, and my foundation…Vada Vad. Thank you for being my greatest cheerleader and supporting me through everything. I love you two more than I can ever explain.

I want to also dedicate this book to my mother, Billie; my late grandfather, Earl; and my two late grandmothers, Vergie and Mattie Pearl. You molded me into the man I am today. I am so grateful for all the valuable lessons you taught me. I love you and I can never, ever repay you.

To the city that made me…Shreveport. I love you 318. From Southern Maid Donuts (the one off of Hearne Ave); to Southern Classic Chicken; to the late Freeman and Harris restaurant. I feel like no other city could have prepared me for life like you have. Shreveport, I will always love you.

Last but not least, to Hip-Hop. I Love You.

Contents

Foreword

He's not going to remember this, but I first met Nick when I was a green-as-hell freshman at the University of Texas in the Fall of 2002. I was walking aimlessly through Jester Dormitory with some fellow Black freshmen when we encountered Nick kicking it with a similar group of upperclassmen. At the time, I thought they were seniors, but I came to find out later that they were just sophomores. I remember being full of anxiety as they approached us. Who knew what these obviously cool upper-classmen would have to say to a square, never-been-away-from-home 18-year-old like myself. I have never been so wrong and full of unnecessary nervousness. Nick and his homies were as welcoming as possible, offering us much advice and kind words. I forgot his name immediately after we left their company. I'm terrible with names. But, I remembered his face and I deeply cherished the interaction. That momentary exchange helped me feel more comfortable in my new and incredibly overwhelming social environment.

Black boys from inner-city environments like "Motown" in Shreveport, Louisiana or the "Southside" of Houston,

Texas often find it difficult to remain their authentic selves while climbing the "ladder of success." Society teaches you that the community that raised you is inadequate, that your dark skin is threatening and that your native tongue is unintelligible.

As such, many of us respond by shedding any signs of "ghetto" life, hoping to quietly assimilate into the dominant culture. Not Nick. Not Nick at all. I first witnessed this when we were both resident assistants. I remember seeing him at resident life meetings, walking around with a big smile on his face, full of young Black male energy. He was hip-hop to his core, from his fashion to his language to the music that pumped from his headphones. He knew he was smart, hardworking and had much to offer the world. Honestly, I looked up to him from a far. I saw him as a true model of Black manhood e v e n though he was barely in his 20s. We're in our 30s now and I still see him this way.

Speaking of Black manhood, African American fraternities often catch much flack. Some say they are elitist, sexist, full of artificial relationships and violent. I spent the first couple of my collegiate years feeling the same way. I was a private person who enjoyed the company of a very small and select group of friends. But, at some point early in my junior year, a member of Alpha Kappa Alpha challenged me to think beyond myself and consider ways that I could serve the campus and the larger Austin community. She suggested joining a fraternity as an option.

Despite initially dismissing the idea, she actually sparked a slight interest that eventually turned into a legitimate desire. I wanted the brotherhood, the collective ideals and I wanted to represent a larger movement as I served the world. I'm not going to lie, I considered other organizations. I had Alphas in my family and I look good in red. But Nick, being a member of Phi Beta Sigma meant a lot to me. He's someone I looked up to and I felt like, since he was cool, the other brothers on campus must be as well. One night, I randomly sent him an email regarding my interest in joining. He never responded. But I pursued it anyway.

The Sigma initiation process allowed me to get to know Nick on a much deeper level. I remember truly bonding with him for the first time when he randomly visited my dorm room. He shared his experiences in fraternity life, asked about my feelings regarding our initiation process and we discussed my college experience in general. We definitely talked about our love for hip-hop, especially our shared Nas fandom.

As you'll see in this memoir, hip-hop has long been a source of empowerment for Nick. The same is true for me. Joining a fraternity is, at the very least, a complicated experience. But similar to our first encounter during my freshman year, Nick provided comfort and security with his words. I became a member of Phi Beta Sigma in the Spring of 2005. Nick was one of my prophytes and I was truly honored to share his line number. What up, Deuce! Blu Phi!

Nick's story is one of incredible trials and remarkable triumphs. It is the account of a young black child born into circumstances that could have led to him becoming a statistic. But the love of a dedicated mother, support from other family members and his own intelligence and resilience enabled him to realize his full potential. Nick is not simply sharing his story out of vanity. Rather, he's using his life to help others navigate this often, treacherous world. As he shares his encounters with poverty, broken homes, gun violence and addiction, Nick teaches us how to interpret and defeat any destructive force that stands in our way.

With *Can U Love Me: A Memoir…A Tribute,* Nicholas Battle gives us the blueprint to find success in a world built for us to fail.

Written with much love and respect,

- Langston Collin Wilkins, PhD.

My brother, Nicholas "Nino" Battle… When I met Nick, the year was 2003. I was on the 5th floor of the athletic dormitory of The University of Texas at Austin's Campus. My twin cousins, Ashton and Aaron Collins, were star track athletes there, in which whom introduced me to Nino. He was the Resident Assistant and the coolest guy to know. Real laid back, down to earth and an intellectual fellow from the Deep South just like the twins and I, so it was no question that we clicked immediately.

At the time, I was going to Concordia University, a private school also located in Austin, Texas, but I would spend most of my days in the UT dorm, roaming the campus, or in the studio about 45 minutes up the road. Nino already knew about my music and would share his opinion and even constructive criticism as needed. I was appreciative of that then and still am today. He's a true friend, always a man of his word, and one you can count on for sure. It is years down the line and Nino's never changed one bit.

Well organized and well groomed, anything Nino does will always be well planned out; which is one of the main reasons why I can't wait to get my copy of this book signed because, far beyond being a brother, I am definitely a fan of the lifestyle decisions my friend makes. Sometimes I borrow from his tenacity and push harder on my own day-to-day grind. He's what we all need, a man of his word. A brother from another, Nino's always been that reliable brother, friend, husband, father, and son. Much love and success bro! Thanks for keeping it real and true with me from Day 1.

- Jerome "Kashflow" Stampley aka SoundsGoodAlready

Preface

As I sit back and reflect on the events that have transpired throughout my life, I realize that my simple beginnings in my hometown of Shreveport, Louisiana are far too familiar in the communities that house children who "look" just like me. Single parent households, coupled with the "crack" epidemic, made life for us 80's babies more challenging than those before us. But, the resiliency of my peers spawned the birth of a generation founded on a hustler's mentality.

Whether the hustle was legal or not, we had to be "go-getters." Sons and daughters had to provide for ourselves due to the disassembly of the family structure our predecessors were accustomed to. It may not have been a perfect situation; however, we made the best of it.

Some of us were fortunate enough to make it out and become America's worst nightmare...an educated, street-smart entrepreneur. Others weren't so fortunate, but the reasoning behind their misfortunes are understandable. Sometimes, the worst option to provide for yourself and your family is the only option presented to you, especially if the foundation of your family unit is as shaky as a nine-month old baby attempting to walk for the first time.

Some of us had no other way out, except for a route that only had one option leading to a path with no light at the end of the tunnel. Equal footing with our crosstown counterparts was hardly ever an option, so we had to force our way into their sophisticated ecosystem. Ruffling feathers or not, we would make our presence known.

The fuel behind my motivation was music, especially Hip-Hop. Scarface taught me why I only saw emotion from a hardened male after a death. 2Pac taught me about the struggles of teen pregnancy within my community. Nas taught me that I can be whatever I want to be because the world is mine. In all honesty, Hip-Hop raised me, and in some instances, Hip-Hop saved my life.

On Tuesday, March 3, 2015, my life changed forever with the birth of my son. Holding him in my arms for the first time, I knew my mission was giving him every opportunity never afforded to me. God willing, I'll do that.

I want my son to understand what I had to endure in order to create the life he's accustomed to. I want him to hear my story from me. No one can reveal my truths except me. So, son, as you read this, just know that your father has come a long way from his beginnings, but my principles and guidelines that I've instilled in you are deeply rooted in our Shreveport foundation. You will feel my pain through these pages, but take in no discouragement from my transgressions. Stay relentless and true to yourself in your pursuit of greatness. As you read this book, I want you to keep an open mind and enjoy the soundtrack to my life. I Love You.

TRACK #1: THE GENESIS

Artist: Nas

Album: Illmatic

(Scan for Apple Song by Artist)

*Nasir Jones created one of the most in-depth and influential rap albums of all time. The Genesis, or the beginning, of this album sets the tone for the project in its entirety; just as this first "Chapter," or should I say "**Track**," does for my entire book.*

Regardless of how this goes down, I gotta keep it real.

In 1983, two family's lives were forever changed through the creation of a young black child, born to two children who did not understand the severity of the situation at hand. My father, Carlos, was a slender and handsome young man that was the apple of his mother's eye. He was the oldest of two sons. His younger brother, Rodney, was a role model to me throughout my years on this earth.

My mother, Billie Renee, was a beautiful and smart woman that was her mother's, Vergie, sixth born child of eight. As with many larger families of that time, the oldest child residing in the home became the surrogate mother to their younger siblings. In this case, my mother helped raise her two younger brothers, Bryant and John-John; two males that would become important figures throughout my life.

It was the week before Christmas of 1982, and my father's parents, Earl and Mattie Pearl, were sitting at their kitchen table. Mattie Pearl was fixing her signature breakfast; grits, eggs, down home sausage, and toast for Earl and the two boys.

"Earl, Carlos, Rodney! Come to the kitchen. Breakfast is ready," she yelled.

My PawPaw Earl sits up in the bed, dressed in nothing

but his grey boxer briefs. "Aww, it's too damn early for this shit," he yawns as he gets up and walks down the hallway leading to the kitchen. He sits down at the table as my grandmother simultaneously brings him his plate. "Mattie Pearl," says PawPaw, "You know I don't eat this without no damn hot sauce."

My grandmother scurried across the kitchen to hand PawPaw his Louisiana hot sauce. She sits down next to her husband and begins to eat.

"Carlos…Rodney," she yelled. "Get yo ass down to the kitchen and eat your breakfast before it gets cold!"

"Yes Ma'am," yells my father. "Rodney," says my father, "How in the hell are we going to tell Momma and Earl?"

"Tell em' what?" My Uncle Rodney said grudgingly.

"About Billie and Daphne," whispers my father. "Man, they're gonna kill us!"

As a few minutes pass by, my PawPaw now begins to yell at the boys.

"If y'all don't bring yo asses to this kitchen, I'm going to come back there and get you myself."

My father and uncle finally get to the table and sit down. My dad begins to eat, but my uncle Rodney is a little hesitant this morning.

"Rodney, what's wrong with you boy?" Earl inquisitively asked.

"Nothing, just tired," replies Rodney as he begins to nibble on the eggs and grits.

As the family continues to eat, my grandmother begins to rattle off a few commands to my PawPaw.

"Earl, I need you to go pick up a cake from Louis' house today for me. I told her you'd be there by 1 o'clock. And when you go to County Market, pick up some mustard greens for dinner tomorrow…"

"Got damn, Mattie Pearl! I got off at 2 this morning," hollered Earl.

"Well…" my grandmother replies before Uncle Rod interrupts.

"Momma, I gotta tell you something," Rodney interjects. My father's eyes peer up from his plate, as he knows his younger brother is about to reveal a truth his parents are unaware of.

"What is it Rodney?" Replies grandma.

"Umm…," he delays.

"Spit it out boy," my grandmother responds.

"Daphne's pregnant…and the baby is due at the end of January," Rodney belts out. A sigh of relief comes over his face, no matter what verbal onslaught my grandmother was going to place on him…and believe me, those verbal lashes were on their way.

"Rodney," yelled Grandma, "What the hell do you mean that Daphne's pregnant? You two are only sixteen. We did not bring you up to go out in these streets making babies. What the hell is wrong with you?"

My grandfather sat speechless. He was already a man of few words, since my grandmother did most of the talking. With his food cooling in front of him, the processing of the heavyweight load of events walked around his mind. My grandma's fussing did not stop.

"Carlos…can you believe your brother," she begins to yell before my father interrupts her.

"Momma," replies my dad with his head down and eyes halfway up. "Billie's pregnant too…and she's due mid-January."

My grandfather's fork dropped to his plate immediately in disbelief. My grandmother was at a loss for words. In fact, her body was at a loss of air as she collapsed in front of her three men. You see, just 10 minutes ago, she was a 41-year-old wife and mother of 2 whose oldest son was 6 months removed from high school graduation, while her youngest son was following the same path, just 2 years behind him. Now she is a two-time grandmother to be, and she only has a few weeks to prepare.

BATTLE'S BLUEPRINT
Adjust to the surprise's life throws at you. What you currently deem as a failure may ultimately become one of your greatest successes.

As my grandmother regains her consciousness, a world of thoughts raced through her head. She was a church going woman, and so were her children. My grandmother treated her sons as kings and expected them to act as that. They were well mannered, well dressed, and hardworking kids that everyone loved within the neighborhood and family. My grandmother adored her children, and many, including family members, took offense to that. Of course, she may have bragged about her sons a little from time-to-time; however, what parents don't do that when they are proud of their children. I will admit, sometimes she could be a little overbearing, but that was just "Mattie Pearl."

After the untimely surprise my grandparents received that morning, my father hurriedly called my mother. As the phone rang, he was relieved, yet timid to tell my mother that the word was out.

"Hello," answered my mom.

"Billie, this is Carlos."

"Hey, what are you doing?"

With a slight hesitation and a stutter, my father stated, "I just told my mom and Earl about the baby…and I think they're on their way to your mom's house now."

"Oh shit…I gotta clean up and tell momma," she replied. "Damn, my momma's not even home yet…Carlos, let me call you back." My mom hangs up the phone and rapidly begins to assure the house is up to Mattie Pearl's standard, who had obsessive compulsive disorder before anyone ever trademarked the name.

"Bryant…John-John, straighten up…NOW! Ms. Brown is on her way!" Yelled my mom.

"What am I going to wear… I need to hurry up…And where the hell is momma?" My mom mused.

As my mom begins to change clothes, Bryant yells out,

"Renee, Mrs. Brown's pulling up!" My mom's heart begins to race as she knows this is the first time in which my father's parents will see her pregnant.

A loud knocking hits the door and my Uncle John-John answers it.

"Hey John-John. Where's Billie?" My grandmother rattles in a semi-rushed voice.

"Yes ma'am..." as he looks awkwardly towards the back of the house. "She's in her room."

Earl and Mattie Pearl walk into the house and my mother emerges from the room in near unison.

"Sooo..." my grandmother ponders, "This is why I haven't seen you in months. Billie, you could have come and talked to us."

My mom hastily replied, "Mrs. Brown, that's not my job. Your son should have told you."

"Well..." replied my grandmother before my PawPaw intervened, "Mattie Pearl...calm it down!" My grandmother throttled back her response, just right before the front door opens.

"Renee, whose car is parked in my front yard?" My mom's mother, Vergie, asked as she scans the room and surprisingly sees my father's parents. "Well, good evening Mr. and Mrs. Brown," says Vergie, in the most condescending voice one can utter, "So Carlos finally decided to acknowledge his future child. You know Renee is due any day now?"

"Mrs. Smith," says Mattie Pearl, not backing down from the verbal warfare challenge, "If we would have known, things would have been different. That's not how we operate."

"Let me make this clear," Vergie stated, "I raised eight kids, mostly by my damn self….and I…we…don't need anything from anyone. This won't be my first grandchild I've had to help raise!"

Cautiously inserting himself into the conversation, my PawPaw steps in, "Vergie, what Mattie Pearl is trying to say is, now that we know a child is coming, we will be here every step of the way from now on."

He reaches his hand out to Vergie and she grabs it to shake.

She quickly responds, "Earl, I'm going to hold you to your word, now."

He acknowledges with a subtle head nod and PawPaw

and Mattie Pearl exit the house and return home.

Joy
Artist: Talib Kweli (Ft Mos Def)
Album: Quality

In the early morning hours of January 15, 1983, my mother woke up with a sharp pain in her stomach that she had never felt before.

"Momma," she says, "This boy won't stop kicking my stomach." She moves from side-to-side in her bed with a slight grimace on her face.

"Girl," shouts Vergie, "Take yo ass back to sleep. We got a busy day ahead of us tomorrow!"

You see, Vergie was an independent woman that did whatever it took to provide for her family. During the daytime, she was a medical laboratory technician at the Louisiana State University Hospital of Shreveport; however, after work, she was a seamstress for nearly every church, friend, or friend-of-a-friend in the city. She sewed almost every church choir robe in Shreveport, made many high school homecoming and prom dresses, and created nearly every article of clothing for all eight of her children. So, waking Vergie up in the wee Saturday morning hours was a brave task, no matter the situation…even the situation that was about to transpire.

"Mommmmmaaaaaa," yelled my mother, "I think I pissed myself!"

A startled Vergie rushed from her bed to my mother's room with an open mouth and raised eyebrows.

"Renee," she says, "He's coming!" "Bryant, get the car ready," she yelled. "Renee's bout to have this baby boy!"

Bryant hops out of his twin-size bed and grabs John-John on his way to getting the keys to the car. Vergie begins to pile whatever she can find into a small duffle bag.

"Mommmmmmaaaa," shouted Renee, "Forget that damn duffle bag…let's go!"

Vergie, with a startled look on her face, screams, "Girl, if you cuss at me one more time…"

Bryant, with an uneasy look on his face, interjects, "Momma, the car is ready…let's go!"

As my family pulls into the Willis Knighton Hospital emergency room entrance, my grandmother jumps out the car to get a wheelchair for my mom. John-John helps her into her seat, off and away. Renee's admittance into the hospital is official now.

"Ma'am, what is your name and date of birth?" The doctor asks.

"Billie Renee Battle...December 9, 1964...and give me a damn epidural!"

About an hour and one epidural later, I entered this world...a young black child born into a situation that, more than likely, results in him becoming a statistic, rather than a success story.

As I lay in my mom's arms, her motherly instincts took over. The immediate connection and bond shared between the two of us was a feeling that even her boisterous manner couldn't describe. She sat in the hospital room next to Vergie and thought of how three generations were side-by-side.

"Renee, what do you think about Christopher?" Vergie says, interrupting my mom's thought pattern.

With an ill look on her face, my mother replies, "Every Chris I know is bad!"

"Well I think I have the perfect name," says my grand-mother. "Seneca...What do you think?"

First off, if you knew Vergie, there's a few things you

knew she loved to do in her spare time. One of them was playing crossword puzzles and the other was watching her daily soap operas when time permitted, especially "Ryan's Hope" of the late 1970s and majority of the 1980s. One of her favorite characters was Dr. Seneca Beaulac; hence the suggestion of "Seneca" for my first name. Now, I'll give Vergie this, Seneca is a quite unique name; however, thank God my mother wasn't having any of that.

"Momma, my baby is not going to be named after a soap star! What about Nicholas?"

Vergie nods in agreement. "But…how about 'Cass' for his middle name?"

With another befuddled look on her face, my mother quickly denounces the name. "Momma, I'm not sure about 'Cass' but I do like 'Jarrell."

The irony of 'Jarrell' is that it is a name also copied from a TV star. My mother arrived at the idea from Superman's (yes, I said Superman) father's name spelled 'Jor-El.' My mother put her own twist to the spelling of Jo-Rel's name and Vergie agreed. I finally had a name.

The doctor and nurse entered the room. "Ms. Battle, do you have a name identified yet for this handsome young man," says the doctor.

My mother wanted a strong name for me, especially since I was born on Dr. Martin Luther King Jr's birthday. Not only did my name have to be strong; however, she understood that life would be substantially harder for me as a young black man. The potentiality of raising a son alone as a single black mother was real. Therefore, my name had to be one that would not immediately identify me as a black male on a future job application. This might sound absurd in today's world, but growing up in the south, especially in Louisiana, minorities had to attempt to "blend in" on paper with their white counterparts in order to have a shot at succeeding in life.

In response to the doctor's question, my mother says with a proud reply, "Nicholas Jarrell Battle!"

"Will the father be signing the certificate today," questions the doctor.

With an uneasy look of her face, she replies, "Do you see him in the room?"

The doctor reciprocates a kind gesture and exits the room.

If you break down my name, you will have an assertion as to why my mother chose each piece. Nicholas comes from the Greek word Nikolaos, meaning "victory of the people." Jarrell comes from a "supernatural" being in "Jor-El," as stated earlier. If you study the history of Superman, you should know that Jor-El is the lead scientist (tuck this nugget away) of the planet Krypton. My last name "Battle" is just a God-given strong name…enough said. Now I do not believe my mother put that much thought into naming me; however, whatever method she chose created a bold name fit for a King…better yet, fit for me.

Where I'm From
Artist: C-Murder (Ft. Prime Suspects)
Album: Life or Death

Shreveport, Louisiana is like many other southern cities across America. My mother grew up in the 1970s in the primarily Caucasian occupied Queensborough neighborhood. In the post-segregation era, black families who could afford to live in predominantly white neighborhoods began to acquire homes in those neighborhoods. The ability to afford their children the opportunity to attend schools in a better school district and better accessibility to the city were conditions that lured these families into neighborhoods that were once unattainable. Black families were no longer subject to housing and educational segregation; and families that had the ability to grant these rights to their children did so in as swift of a manner as possible.

Many middle-class black families, forced to live in segregated neighborhoods, grew tired of living with inequality. These upwardly mobile African-Americans were now migrating into prominent middleclass white neighborhoods to achieve a sense of accomplishment. The desire for a sense of providing a better life for their family grew. My grandmother Vergie, and her late husband John, were one of these black families that had the ability to make such a move.

As hard working-class black families, like Vergie and John, began to move in these neighborhoods, some of the white families that harbored the pre-integration era racially charged sentiments immediately moved out, creating a situation termed "white flight." As my mother grew older, the neighborhood became more "black," to the point where one would believe that we were experiencing segregation all over again.

My mother grew up on Catherine Street; a long, straight and narrow road that connected two major city thoroughfares: Jewella and Hearne Avenues. The trees within the community were mature and beautiful. Residents had respectable jobs within the community, drove nice vehicles, and kept well-manicured lawns. Mrs. Griffin, whose daughter Alicia was one of my mother's best friends, was a school teacher. Mr. and Mrs. Nunn were both factory workers at the thriving AT&T plant in Shreveport. Their daughter, Daphne, was another best friend of my mother, and default aunt and God-mother to me. If you recall from earlier, my father's brother, Rodney, and Daphne were set to have a child nearly two weeks after my due date.

Queensborough seemed to have it all. It was a peaceful and beautiful neighborhood that black families, who once could never imagine having the opportunity to live in, were proud and flourishing residential home owners.

The Mooretown community is where my father grew up. My grandparents, Earl and Mattie Pearl, bought their house in 1969 and resided in the home the remainder of their lives. The Mooretown community is historically important within the Shreveport community. Formed in the early 1900s by Giles D. Moore, African Americans developed a thriving independent society. Originally run entirely by black people, the community and its occupants have remained predominantly black since its inception.

Although Mooretown, or Motown as us natives like to call it, is majority black, many prominent individuals have come from this community such as NFL players, city councilmen, doctors, lawyers, and military officers. The Motown community's foundational rock rests upon a place built *brick-by-brick* for black people, and occupied by blacks. Therefore, the need for "white flight" never materialized. Instead, it was a haven for blacks to have the opportunity to own their "little" piece of the American dream.

Francis Street, the street my father grew up on, was a small-knit 'community within a community' of Motown; comprising of two cul-de-sacs and only twenty-one homes. The next-door neighbors were Mr. Wilson and Mrs. Wilson, a couple that I always looked at as an additional set of grandparents. The other neighbor's original name was Mr. Easter, until he later converted to The Nation of Islam and changed his name to Abumentee. He was an independent hustler by nature…and no, I'm not talking about moving weight. He did various jobs that allowed him to provide himself enough funds to not work or answer to anyone.

He sold cassette tapes, incents, potpourri, and just about anything you needed under a nearby bridge just a few miles from my grandparent's house. In fact, Abumentee sold me my first cassette tapes I ever had; MC Lyte – "Act Like You Know" and J.J. Fad – "Supersonic." Down the street, lived Mr. and Mrs. Frasier, a factory worker and elementary school teacher, respectively. Across the street was Mr. Rogers, another hard-working middleclass man.

When my father grew up, Motown was a thriving community that hard-working, decent families could afford a nice house in a neighborhood that was safe for their children. Every house had home owners that showed great pride within their community. There were even unofficial Christmas light decoration contests that, although I'm biased, my grandmother won every year. All-in-all, Motown was a pseudo All-American neighborhood in an "unconventional" way by American standards.

Queensborough and Mooretown are neighborhoods

that are less than 3 miles away from each other. Both communities used the same grocery stores, pharmacy, meat market, cleaners, etc. Both neighborhood's students also fed into the same high school feeder pattern.

The school referenced is Fair Park High School. Prior to desegregation, Fair Park was a high school zoned for white students. Post integration, Fair Park became a "mixed" school that encompassed multiple nationalities, to include blacks, whites, and Hispanics. This environment cultivated talents that are known across the country. Fair Park High School produced two Louisiana House of Representative members in Roy Brun and Rick Edmonds; a Pulitzer Prize winning journalist in Stanley Tiner; a Lieutenant General of the United States Air Force in Tome Walters, Jr; a national television broadcaster in Tim Brando; an Olympic silver and bronze medalist in Hollis Conway, and numerous professional athletes across many sports. Fair Park brought many people from different backgrounds and neighborhoods together. It fostered an environment where a young lady from Queensborough and a young man from Motown could meet. The rest is history.

The Foundation
Artist: Xzibit
Album: At the Speed of Life

I arrived at my Grandmother Vergie's house in Queensborough just two days after my mother gave birth to me. As my mother steps out of the car with me in her arms, she faces the house and realizes that reality is about to set in. Before my mother found out she was pregnant, she was, not only one of the smartest students of her class, but also one of the most popular. She graduated as salutatorian of her class, resulting in multiple scholarship awards to a few Louisiana colleges. She was also a majorette in the Fair Park High School Marching Band. She was beautiful, talented and smart; what most would call a triple threat.

My mother had big dreams of going off to college and making it out of "small-town" Shreveport, but my emergence derailed those plans immediately. As a child, I sometimes wondered if my mother ever regretted not being able to capitalize on her talents earlier in her life because of me. But, in true "mom" fashion, she would always reassure me in so many ways that I was her only blessing in life that she never regretted, but rather welcomed the challenges that we were going to face…together.

After a couple of weeks of acclimating to becoming a parent, the house phone begins to ring.

"John-John," yells my mom. "Pick up the phone."

"Hello," John-John answers in a happily and childish voice.

"Is this John-John?" Asks the caller.

"Yes Ma'am," he replies.

"This is Mrs. Brown," my grandmother states. "Where's Renee?"

John-John rushes to my mother's room to tell her to come to the phone and speak to Mrs. Brown.

"Hello, Mrs. Brown," my mother replies.

"Hey Renee," says my grandmother in an optimistic tone, "Earl and I wanted to know if we could see the baby this weekend? Just for a few hours, if that's alright with you," suggests Mattie Pearl.

My mother agrees and converses with my grandmother a few more minutes before the two politely end the call. This was a big moment for my mother and I. For one, this would be the first time in my infant years that I would not be glued to my mother's hip. Secondly, the formal introduction to my Motown grandparents had to take place. Their combined help was instrumental with my mother raising me for the remainder of my childhood years.

"Carlos," fusses my grandmother. "Grab that blanket from the laundry room and bring it outside."

"Yes ma'am," says my father as he looks over to my Uncle Rodney and whispers, "You're next...."

"Rodney," she shouts again. "Bring me a glass of water please."

My uncle looks at my father and chuckles before belting out, "You want a big cup or small cup momma?"

"Boy!" Hollers Mattie. "Stop playing and bring me a big glass of water before Renee gets here!"

My grandmother grabs the blanket my father gave her and spreads it in her front yard. She carefully and meticulously lays the blanket completely flat, with each edge smoothed down in perfect position. The large magnolia tree in the front yard stands perfectly trimmed. Mattie's caladiums were in full bloom with their red veins shining bright. Yellow, orange, white, and pink daffodils outlined the flower box, perfectly accenting the bold caladiums. The grass was a dark hunter green that my grandmother watered daily for at least two hours every night. Two pear trees lined the neatly trimmed sidewalk. While my grandmother's yard always stood as one to behold, today it is the perfect backdrop for an impromptu photoshoot.

My grandparent's home was just five houses down from the corner. As my mother turned down Francis Street in Vergie's white Mercury, Mattie Pearl noticed immediately and sprung to her feet as if an important dignitary was parking in her yard. My mother pulls the car in the driveway, slowly stops, and places the car in park. As she turns the car off, my father and uncle step out the front door. My mother exits the vehicle and walks around to the rear of the car.

"Man, go help her get the baby," whispers my uncle with a nudge to my father.

My dad reaches in the back and removes me from my car seat.

"Hey boo boo…baby," he says in the most *parentish* voice ever. He holds me close and looks at me in my little brown baby eyes. A rush of emotion and thoughts stream through his heart and mind as he realizes that half of me is an exact replication of himself. My dad, still holding me tight, glances over at my grandmother.

"Carlos," says my grandmother. "Look at him…he's got your eyes!"

With a sarcastic chuckle in his voice, my dad says, "Well, if he has my eyes, then he and I both got them honestly."

"Boy," she replies. "Put my baby on that blanket and bring that outfit I bought him outside."

My grandmother changes me into this powder blue and white outfit and sits me up on a pillow propped on her white blanket. She takes out a camera and begins to take pictures.

"Carlos, make sure he doesn't fall over," she tells my dad.

"Ok, Momma," he replies. "I got him."

Uncle Rodney looks at them both and begins to laugh as he knows my grandmother is beginning to irritate my dad. To absorb some of my grandmother's and dad's humorous agitation, my uncle inserts himself into their conversation.

"Momma," he says. "When is Earl coming home?"

"Earl will be home soon. He just stopped by Super-1 to

pick up some groceries for dinner tonight," she replies.

As if my PawPaw's ears were ringing from hearing his name, he turns down Francis Street on his way to the house. He parks his car on the street and rushes over to my dad.

"Carlos," says Earl. "Let me see that boy!"

My dad hands me over to my PawPaw with a smile on his face. Earl looks at me and then looks at my grandmother with a smile from ear-to-ear.

"Mattie Pearl," he says, "I think we got a winner here," he chuckles

"Haha," she replies. "Yes, Earl we do."

"Rodney," my PawPaw replies. "Get those groceries out of the car and bring them in the house. It's time to go for a ride!"

As my uncle does what's instructed, my PawPaw gets in the car and puts me in his lap. He starts the car up and begins to drive down Francis Street. He begins honking the horn and neighbors begin to come outside.

"Earl," says a close neighbor down the street. "What in the hell is all that honking for?"

"Cleve," with a grin on his face "I'm a grandfather now and this is a winner right here boy!"

Mr. Cleveland nods and tips his hat in congratulatory spirits towards my grandfather. Earl continues to drive through Motown, honking his horn and announcing me to the neighborhood. After about ten minutes of this, he returns home to everyone moving in a panic and frenzy.

"What the hell is wrong with y'all?" Earl asks. "This is a celebration!"

"It's Daphne," replies my Uncle Rodney. "She's going into labor…we gotta get to the hospital…NOW!"

"Mr. Brown," my mother says. "I'll take Nicholas back to my house and y'all can go to the hospital."

In a frantic voice, my PawPaw agrees and then directs the rest of the family to pile in the car. Earl, Mattie Pearl, Carlos, and Rodney make their way towards the hospital, while my mother makes her way back to her home in Queensborough. As my mother makes it home, my Aunt Daphne goes into labor and eventually has her first son, my cousin and "brother," Jay.

Although unexpected, Earl and Mattie Pearl became grandparents two times over in a thirteen-day span. With Jay and I being born so close in such a close timeframe, we made our journey throughout life together with much guidance from the three families that were able to experience a lifetime of joy due to their two new additions. From this point on, life was never the same.

TRACK #2: WHY

Artist: Jadakiss

Album: Kiss of Death

Mr. "Top 5 Dead or Alive" asked a lot of relevant questions in this song that relate to life as I saw it in Shreveport. My questions I had were similar.

"Why did crack have to hit so hard?"
"Why is there a murder every-other day of the week?"
"Why do my people have to work so hard to get on a level playing field?"

The year is 1990. My father joined the Navy 6 years earlier, just before my second birthday, leaving the city of Shreveport and relocating to Oregon. As a youth, I was proud to say that my dad was a Navy-man. It brought me joy, not that he was in the Navy, but that I could speak of what my dad was doing and who he was. Today, as an adult and father, I look at that situation completely different. The thought of leaving my only son without his father scares me. As a father, I am my son's superhero; the man he should strive to be like. Growing up with a father in your life should yield fruitful memories that you will be able to communicate to your children and future generations. Those memories never materialized due to my dad's actions.

As I look back at my life, I can't be mad at him for leaving. He felt he needed to leave to make his life better, and in turn, that would make my life better also. However, as much as I love my dad, his absence throughout some of my biggest moments and accomplishments in life still haunt me to this day.

Although I had the best mother a child could ever ask for, a son needs his father present in his life to show him how to navigate through this cold world. Instead, my mom was both my mother and father. She played football with me…she shot basketballs with me…she enrolled me in swimming lessons, basketball camps, and summer football programs. My mother did everything she could to keep my mind occupied in an effort to keep me focused and avoid the temptations of wavering to the dark sides of life. She guided me through this world and put me in the absolute best possible situations to succeed.

As my father was able to move freely and change goals and life plans whenever he chose, my mother did not have that freedom. She had one mission in life, and that was to groom and teach a young black boy to become a man. For a single mother, this proved to be a difficult task; however, if anyone was up to this feat, it was Billie Renee Battle. Life finally settled in for her. The luster of a new baby completely wore off, and she was now in 100 percent single parent mode.

By this time in life, my mother was still living with my grandmother Vergie, who had moved from her house in Queensborough to another house in the Motown community, less than two miles away from Earl and Mattie Pearl's house. The house was cozy, especially with the amount of family members my grandmother housed. Under one roof, there was my grandmother, her husband John (PawPaw John), my mother, Bryant, John-John, my cousin BC, and, finally, me.

We were a tight knit unit. PawPaw John worked in the oil industry. As stated earlier, grandma Vergie was a Miss "do-it-all" with three to four jobs at all times. My uncle John-John was more like an older brother to me than an uncle. BC was like an older sister. Bryant was the cool uncle that would let me do anything my mother would never let me think of doing. He let me eat candy all day, drink cokes, and let me cuss when no one was around. My uncle was truly the life of the party. That house, in my eyes, was always full of joy. Although we did not have much, we had each other. That is what made it so special to me.

Growing Up in the Hood
Artist: Compton's Most Wanted
Album: Straight Checkin' 'Em

Mattie Pearl was a school teacher at Lakeshore

Elementary in the Queensborough neighborhood. My neighborhood was zoned for attendance at another school. My grandmother circumvented that rule, enrolling me in the school she taught at easing my mother's burden. You see, even though my dad was not physically present in my life as one would want, his parents did a lot of his "heavy lifting" when it came to me. With my grandparents now living in the same neighborhood, I was able to nearly equally divide my time spent between the two households.

My grandmother Mattie and PawPaw Earl greatly respected my mother because she embodied the mature qualities that they would have loved to see if they would have had a daughter. Just two years after my Uncle Rod was born, my grandmother and Earl were set to have another child. My grandmother carried the baby just long enough to be able to identify its sex. Astounded and excited, my grandmother had great joy in learning she was going to have a baby girl. Just a few weeks after hearing the news, my grandmother had a miscarriage. She would speak on the incident from time-to-time. Her mood would become less vibrant and resemble that of a somber soul. As a child, my grandmother would always say my mother was the daughter she never had. As I got older and was able to comprehend my grandmother's words, I began to understand the true level of appreciation she and my PawPaw held for my mother.

"Ding…Ding…Ding," rang the school bell. It was the last day of my first-grade year at Lakeshore. I jolted out of Ms. Bank's classroom into the hallway to get to my grandmother's room. The mob of students cluttered the hallways, creating no line of sight to my destination. With a dazed look on my face, I see my grandmother's best friend and fellow school teacher, Mrs. Frazier.

"Nicholas," she states in her boisterous voice, "Your grandmother went to the teacher's lounge."

"Yes ma'am…Thank you" I replied.

I rushed to the teacher's lounge as if I were Emmitt Smith running towards an end zone. "Grandma," I said as I reached the lounge. "You ready?"

"Where's your manner's boy?"

"I'm sorry," I replied as I veered towards my grandmother's colleagues. "Hi Mrs. Nickels…Hi Mrs. Coleman."

They both spoke to me and persisted to continue small talk amongst each other. My grandmother joined into the conversation and belted out a large laugh, probably due to something funny Mrs. Nickels said. As the three finish up their conversation, my grandmother tells me to get my bookbag as we head out to her white Lincoln Continental. We enter the car and head off to my grandmother's house.

"Nicholas, did you enjoy school this year?"

"Yes Ma'am."

"What did you like about it most?"

"Learning numbers in Mrs. Banks' class."

"Ok…what else?"

"Well," I thought, "I liked a few of my friends. I liked Mrs. Frazier's P.E class."

Sometimes, I couldn't understand why my grandmother would ask me school questions. I was a straight 'A' student that didn't cause any problems in school. I listened, I learned, and I applied myself to completing my schoolwork; although, I really had no choice in the matter. My grandmother was very strict with my cousin Jay and I, as it pertained to school. She had us both reading at a fifth-grade level before ever stepping foot in our second-grade classroom. My grandmother received her Bachelor's Degree from Grambling University and her Master's Degree from Centenary College. Understanding the benefits of achieving a college education, she wanted us to be afforded those same benefits as well.

BATTLE'S BLUEPRINT

Learning is not only a classroom experience. To fully digest the material, you must have open dialogue to promote better insight into the subject matter.

We finally arrive at my grandmother's house. I walk over to the refrigerator and get a cold Country Time canned lemonade before going to the kitchen counter to grab a glazed lemon cookie. I proceed to the den, sit on one of the barstools they had in the room, and begin to indulge in my snack before my grandmother comes into the room.

"Shotgun," she says. "Am I bringing you home tonight, or are you staying with us?"

"I want to stay here tonight and see PawPaw."

"Boy," she snickers. "You and your PawPaw. Well, call your mom and ask her if it's fine for you to spend the night."

"Yes Ma'am."

I go into my grandparent's kitchen and call my other

grandmother's house. My mother answers the phone.

"Hello," she answers.

"Hey Mom."

"You ready for me to pick you up."

"I kinda wanted to stay here tonight," I replied. "I need to get a haircut and PawPaw's going to Big Ben's tomorrow to get his hair cut. I need to get a haircut too so…"

"Ok…I'll come by tomorrow evening to get you."

"Ok. Thanks momma…love you."

"Love you too."

As I hang up the phone, a big smile came across my face. I loved staying at my grandmother Mattie and PawPaw's house. It was like a tranquil sense of peace for me. They had a three-bedroom house in Motown with two full baths. That might not mean much to many of you, but coming from where I'm from, it was a game changer because my "everyday" life resided with my mother, under the roof of my grandmother Vergie.

By this time, my grandmother Vergie moved from her house in Motown to the Village Square apartment complex in the nearby Hollywood Heights neighborhood. Her husband, my PawPaw John, had recently passed away. My grandmother suffered a stroke a few years earlier, causing paralysis in half of her body. Her unfortunate turn of health created an environment where she was no longer able to work and provide for her family as she once did. Forced to downsize our living situation, a 2-bedroom, 1-bathroom first floor apartment became necessary. At times, up to six people were living in close quarters.

The change in our living situation was drastic. We had plenty of love; however, looking back on the situation, our conditions and accommodations weren't the greatest. The apartment buildings were heavily infested with roaches. I remember instances where I would go into the cabinet to grab the Rice Crispy cereal box to get some breakfast before school. As I'd open the cereal, two or three roaches would scatter. I'd pour my cereal into the bowl without a care in the world, and sift it around to make sure none of them made it into my bowl. Then, I'd pour my milk and consume my meal. It might seem crazy, but growing up, that was normal. My mental mind state became immune to that. You either ate or went to school hungry. This was my reality. I say this to not disparage my grandmother. I only say this to show the varying situations that a child that looks like me, and experienced life as I did, had to encounter on a day-to-day basis. The material things, or lack thereof, didn't matter. The hierarchal family structure, composed of three generations under one roof, is what made life beautiful within Vergie's house.

For everything my grandmother Vergie's apartment was, Earl and Mattie's house was its antithesis. With a two-income household, they were able to buy nearly anything they wanted in their home. With my grandmother's OCD-like behavior, she maintained a near flawless house. Everything was in place. Kitchen table placemats perfectly centered in front of each chair around the table were a must. Every morning, bed making happened immediately after waking up. Floor vacuuming occurred every day and no dishes were ever left dirty in the sink. My grandparent's house was the "model" home for organization and order...and I enjoyed the structure. She was a fusser; however, if you kept her house the way she liked it, she would never bother you.

Earl and Mattie's house stood as a symbol of stability for me. The location however, remained unmoved. It did not matter how much money they spent within the home to keep it near immaculate. As stated earlier, Motown was a 99-percent African American community. Although there were many hard-working middleclass black families living here, there were also an abundance of lower income families residing in our neighborhood, mainly due to the segregated zoning areas created just a few decades earlier.

During the 1940s – 1960s, most blacks had to live in our "own" neighborhoods, no matter your financial situation. Decades later, this created an environment where single family homes resided next to low income Section 8 apartment buildings.

Living life as a lower income resident sometimes created situations where individuals had to find other means to acquire funds more quickly to survive. For this reason, it's not a secret that much illegal activity happened in Motown. Drug dealing, prostitution, home invasions, auto theft, and murder occurred in Motown at a much higher rate than other neighborhoods within Shreveport. During the mid-1980s, at the initiation of the crack cocaine epidemic, the Motown community, like many others saw an uptick in this illegal activity that would shake its residents to their core.

U Hear Dat
Artist: Soulja Slim
Album: Years Later...A Few Months After

Finally, school finished for the year. My grandmother Mattie and I sat in the den and watched TV together. Every night, she would watch her pre-recorded VHS tapes of her favorite soap opera, "The Young and the Restless," as well as recordings of horse racing from the Louisiana Downs horse racing track and casino in nearby Bossier City. I could never get into the soap operas she watched, but I did love to see the horse racing. We'd sit down and bet against each other, as to which horse would win the race.

"Shotgun," shouted Mattie. "Which one do you have winning?"

"The grey-looking horse with spots."

"Well, I got the all-brown horse."

We'd watch the TV with anticipation for the horse gates to open and see the huge animals bolt out running. My horse bolted out to a slight lead, but eventually lost to a faster black horse. My grandmother and I looked at the horses for a while before she got tired and went to her room to go to sleep. I stayed up and went to my Uncle Rodney's room to play Zelda on Nintendo before going to sleep myself.

"Boom, Boom, Boom, Boom," was the sound I heard round 1:13 AM. I vaguely remember waking up to the gunshots heard just a few streets over. The shootings were becoming clearer to hear at night, suggesting that they were getting closer by the day.

To say this sound was unusual would be to offer a lie to the reader. As Motown citizens, you became accustomed to hearing shots at night, whether it be from a Glock 45 or AK-47. You quickly learned to desensitize your emotions to the sounds because if you woke up to every shot you heard, you'd never get any sleep, especially considering Shreveport's murder rate was more than five times the national average.

Although the gunshots didn't always wake me up, one thing that did was my grandmother's breakfast. Scrambled eggs, Down Home sausage, cheese grits, and Nature's Own wheat toast was her go-to breakfast meal. The savory aroma woke me up every Saturday morning, no matter what.

I rush to the bathroom and brush my teeth before

washing my face. I proceed into the kitchen to sit in my normal spot. PawPaw gets up and walks down to the kitchen also. He just got home a few hours earlier after pulling a 14-hour shift at the battery plant. Grandma slides our plates in front of us both and we begin eating before hearing the doorbell ring. My grandma peers out the door and sees Leon, an ex-Vietnam veteran whose life had succumb to abusing crack cocaine.

"Mrs. Brown," he says. "Did you hear those shots last night? These niggas are getting closer and closer."

"Naw, I didn't hear it Leon. You must have been out and about last night?"

"Yes Ma'am," he replied. "I heard it as I was walking back to my momma's house."

"Ok."

"Do you need any help around your yard today Mrs. Brown?"

"Yea," replied my grandmother. "You can rake my leaves for me."

"Yes Ma'am," replied Leon as he scurried to the side of the house to retrieve the rake to begin his work.

Although many looked down upon Leon because of his

lifestyle, my grandmother would always help him out by giving him small side jobs to earn a little money. Whether it was raking leaves, pulling weeds from my grandmother's flower bed, or just simply watering her yard; my grandmother always had a soft spot for Leon. She knew he had problems, as she had seen his declining transformation throughout the years.

Everyone in the neighborhood knew and understood Leon's drug problems with crack. It was the epidemic that was sweeping though the poor, minority neighborhoods across America. Motown used to be a neighborhood for thriving blacks; however, now with the emergence of crack, the quality of life within the neighborhood had swiftly declined for the worst.

Young children who were not yet old enough to get a job had an opportunity to make money. They had an opportunity to provide their single mother's with funds to help around the house. As wrong as it may seem, this was their chance to become the "man" of the house, and they relished in this opportunity.

As the demand for crack increased, these youth began to make a lot of money very fast. With a new surplus of flowing money, protection, in the form of pistols, knives, and revolvers became an accessory to your everyday wardrobe; creating a volatile environment that initial Motown residents were not accustomed to.

Property left to children from their parent's after their deaths became dope houses…or as my Atlanta brethren might call it…trap houses. What once was a warm and inviting neighbor's house was becoming a gathering spot for drug dealers and users to exchange dope for money and habitat. Children became dealers. Parents became users. Some children even served dope to their own parents. Motown had taken a complete 180 degree turn from the once thriving community my grandparents raised their children in. It was now becoming a neighborhood that many tried to avoid…a neighborhood that many were now beginning to fear.

Murder
Artist: UGK
Album: Ridin' Dirty

During the summer following my first-grade year, I

made a new friend by the name of Charles. He was about 4 years older than the rest of us; however, Charles gravitated to the younger kids on the block, just as much as we gravitated towards him. Honestly, he probably enjoyed being a mini "leader" around us because we all looked up to him. One thing Charles could do was play basketball well. I was never really a basketball player, but I'd go to the courts up the street from the house to play a few pick-up games with him.

One morning, Charles came by the house to see if I wanted to go catch a few games with him, like always.

With a knock on my grandmother's screen door, my PawPaw comes up to the front to answer the door.

"What's up Charles?"

"Hey Mr. Brown. Can Nick come out and play?"

"Nicholas," yelled PawPaw.

I walked to the front from my room in the back. I grab my shoes next to the door, while my PawPaw goes to sit back down in his usual spot on the couch.

"We going to the park?" I asked Charles.

"Yea...let's go," he replied as I grabbed my shoes.

We walked up to the park, right across the street, on the

corner of Kennedy and Henry Street. We hooped a few games before going back to Francis St.

"Charles, you coming out tomorrow?"

"You know it!"

"Aight bro…see you then."

I walk into my granny's house and Charles went into his house. It was a manufactured home cattycornered from my grandmother and PawPaw's house…right on the corner of Francis and Kennedy.   This house always appeared to be the most "run down" house in the neighborhood. Its occupants were typically a lower income family. Charles and his family were probably the fourth family to live there in five years. That house witnessed constant rotation, and the family that lived there usually sold drugs out of the house. It became normal practice for that house in Motown.

Around this time in my life, the Los Angeles gang culture had migrated outside of California and made its way east and south across America. During the 1950s and 1960s, many Southern black families traveled west to Los Angeles due to the emerging factory jobs within that area. In fact, my PawPaw's mother left Shreveport and moved to Los Angeles, settling in a few places while there, mainly in

Compton and Watts until she passed away in 2010. With the emergence of the LA gang culture, specifically the Crips and Bloods, teens would find themselves in neighborhood feuds that would often result in violence. On some occasions, the LA families would send their kids back to the south to get away from the gang activity that was plaguing them for years. Small towns like Shreveport; Jackson, Mississippi; and Little Rock, Arkansas were the homes of those migrated families, so grandparents and aunts became the new surrogate parents for some of these gang members.

With a fresh start in life and new turf to roam, Crip and Blood sets began to pop up quite frequently in these areas. Shreveport was no different. When I was growing up, it was easy to point out local gangs in the area. You had Hoovers, Crip sets, and Blood sets that I could remember. Charles was a Crip and he looked the part. Between the Dickie and Ben Davis pants, blue t-shirt, and Cortez Nikes with blue laces, his affiliations were clear on sight. He didn't cause too much trouble on the street, though. He was respectful to the elders and only got out of line when people took it "there" with him. Honestly, he was just a pretty good dude until you pushed his buttons.

The morning after our basketball games was a day I'll never forget. It was a hot summer day, so hot that the concrete driveways h a d ripples of heat venting upwards from it. I walked down the street to hit up Charles about the plan for the day. It was still early so we decided to meet up a little later. I go inside the house and watch some TV with my PawPaw before we begin to hear a loud commotion outside. My PawPaw and I walk outside to see what all the fuss was about. To my displeasure, my PawPaw just walked outside with some jeans, flip-flops, and shirtless. I just remember telling him to put a shirt on and he laughed at me as I was speaking. Once we get outside, we see someone dressed in all red yelling at Charles.

"Bitch ass nigga," the person said. "Come catch this fade!"

"I don't fight no bitches," screamed Charles. "Take yo bitch ass home girl!"

"Yo mama a bitch…scary ass nigga!"

At that moment, I realized that this was not going to turn out well for anyone involved. If you knew Charles, you understood his family dynamic. His mother was in jail for drug possession and his uncle was raising Charles, along with Charles' other siblings and his own children. To talk about Charles' mom is to ask for a straight ass whoopin' or worse. An anger in Charles' demeanor was present from that moment on. He started walking towards the girl and spouting more shit to her.

"Leave my mama up out of this hoe!"

"Oh, you a mama's boy, huh nigga!"

Charles begins to walk faster towards the girl. My PawPaw saw exactly what was about to transpire.

"Nicholas," he said. "Go in the house."

"But PawPaw…"

"Go in the house, I said!"

I began to walk to the door before hearing a loud BOOM…BOOM! The girl had shot twice at Charles, missing both times. I ran back to the front to stand next to my PawPaw as we looked at this craziness. Charles ran back into the house as his uncle opened the door. The girl was still shooting at the house and walking closer, hoping to get a better shot on Charles; however, she was too late. Charles emerged from the house with a shotgun. He cocked it once. *BOOM!* He cocked it again. *BOOM!* The sound was deafening as it was so close to the house.

The girl fell to the ground, shaking as she neared death. Charles ran back into the house, just realizing a bullet grazed his lower left leg. His uncle began screaming at him.

"Get the fuck in the house…give me the gun!"

"Aight…Unc I'm hit!"

"You straight," he assures Charles as he looks at the wound. "You need to get the fuck up out of here. The cops gonna be here soon."

Charles takes heed to what his uncle says and begins to run from the house. He hopped Ms. Wilson's fence and then proceeded to the neighbor's yard behind her, where he lost one of his shoes. As this occurs, the ambulance came to the scene and eventually pronounced the girl dead on arrival. We didn't know where exactly Charles went, but the police picked him up after some time passed. I guess he was the only brother in the neighborhood walking around with only one shoe.

Everyone began to wander outside to watch what was happening in front of us, mainly out of shock. Although Motown was not known to be the best of neighborhoods, bad things were not supposed to happen on Francis Street…the little secluded cul-de-sac within the hood. This street was quiet…or so we thought. Sure, people saw drug deals made on the street daily; however, the dead end and cul-de-sac didn't allow for normal foot traffic on our block. It was a mini haven for us locals. At that moment, whatever "manufactured" innocence our street had was gone. We were no different than any other part of Motown, although we had a false misconception of our current reality.

BATTLE'S BLUEPRINT
Do not become a victim of your environment…outgrow it.
Your environment does not shape your reality.

After that day, I never saw Charles again. I never learned what happened to him. He probably went to juvenile and got out eventually due to his age. His uncle moved from the house about three months later, with no trace of where he was going. A few weeks later, another family moved into the house as if nothing happened. It was what we would now become accustomed to.

Kick in the Door
Artist: Notorious B.I.G.
Album: Life After Death

Motown was getting worse. My grandmother Vergie's apartment complex in Hollywood Heights was getting rougher by the day as well. The school systems in each neighborhood were not up to my mother's standards for her only child. She wanted better for me, but did not know how to give me the access to a better life she desired for me. This wasn't the first or the last time, but my mother felt backed into a corner not knowing how to get us out of it.

I was due to start my second-grade school year in the upcoming month. My mother began to scope out schools she would love for me to attend. My grandmother Vergie had this huge blue Ford Galaxy that my mom would drive when looking at schools. We passed by multiple schools before eventually coming to Southern Hills Elementary. It was a majority white school; however, there were a few black students there that wouldn't make me feel out of place if I were able to attend.

This school was so far away from where I lived, though.

With no idea on how I could be eligible to attend classes here, my mother had to do something drastic. She parked the Galaxy in the school's parking lot and sits silent for a minute. As she breaks her moment of silence, my mom begins to mentally go over her plan of action.

As my mom starts to get out the car, she says to me, "Nicholas…let's go."

"What are we doing mom?"

"Just come on."

We enter the main staff front office.

"May I help you ma'am," requests the secretary.

"Who do I need to speak to concerning enrollment into the school for my son?"

"Mrs. Cox is our principal," the secretary replies, "but she's currently away from the office. Would you like a bus route and schedule?"

"Actually, we're not zoned for this district."

"Well ma'am, if you do not live in this district, your child will be unable to attend this school."

Interrupting the secretary hastily, my mother responds, "I understand that but when is Ms. Cotts…Ms. Cox returning back to the office?"

"She went to lunch. You can sit in our waiting area until she returns if you'd like."

My mother accepts the gesture and brings me over to the waiting area where we sit down. I was confused. I thought I would be going back to school at Lakeshore where my grandmother taught. I could not understand what was going on.

"Momma, why do I have to go to school here?"

"Nicholas, this is a really good school and a really good opportunity for you."

"But Momma, I like going to school with my grandmother."

With a direct voice towards me, my mother says, "Baby, this is a great move for you. You might not understand the importance of this now, but you will in due time."

A grey-haired white woman in her late 40s entered the office. She walked with an air of confidence that immediately drew you to her. She spoke loudly, but with a soft voice. Her secretary beamed with joy as she began to speak.

"What do we have on the calendar for the remainder of the day," relayed Ms. Cox.

"Ma'am, you have a 2 P.M. appointment with the Turner

Middle School Principal. He'll be in the area and just wanted to stop by and chat for a while."

"Ok…easy enough"

With an uneasy look on her face, my mother semi-loudly cleared her voice.

"Excuse me ma'am," stated my mother.

In a hurriedly fashion, the secretary interjects, "Oh yes, Ms.Cox. You have a visitor regarding enrollment for the fall."

With her hand extended, the principal introduces herself, "Linda Cox…How may I help you ma'am?"

With a firm handshake, my mother replies, "Billie Battle, and this is my son Nicholas. How are you?"

"I'm fine Ms. Battle. What can I do for you today?"

"I am here to setup my son's enrollment process for the fall semester."

"Simple enough," replied Ms. Cox with a smile. "Have you talked to my secretary? She can get you all the forms to get little Nicholas here squared away."

"Ma'am," replied the secretary, "Ms. Battle does not live in our district. Per the zoning rules, her son is not allowed to attend this school."

"Ms. Battle," stated Ms. Cox, "If this is true, then the information provided by my secretary is correct. I'm truly sorry."

With an eager voice, my mother instructed me to sit down in the waiting area while she talked to Ms. Cox. I obeyed, took my seat, and picked up a *"Clifford the Red Dog"* book sitting on the console table next to the chair. My mother begins to converse with Ms. Cox about the situation.

"Ms. Cox, is there any way my son can attend this school?"

"Ms. Battle, by the rules and guidelines placed in front of me, I cannot. Again, I'm sorry to deliver this bad news."

"But ma'am, he's a gifted child. He'll be starting the second grade, but is already reading at a fifth-grade level. He..."

"Ms. Battle," says Ms. Cox, "I simply cannot. I'm sorry."

"Well Ms. Cox, I understand," my mother replies. "However, I want you to personally tell my son that...just so he understands why. You can better explain it than I..."

"But Ms. Battle....," says Ms. Cox.

"Nicholas," my mother replies as she cuts Ms. Cox off

mid-sentence. "Come speak to Ms. Cox before we leave."

"Yes ma'am," I replied. I placed the book down, rose from the chair, and walked towards Ms. Cox.

"Nicholas," said Ms. Cox, "I…I…come into my office."

I followed Ms. Cox to her office and sat down in one of the chairs in front of her desk as she begins to speak to me.

"So, Nicholas, what's your favorite subject?"

"Math. I love math…multiplying and dividing is awesome!"

"What else do you like?"

"I love dinosaurs also," I replied. "In April, I was featured as the 'Student of the Week' on TV."

"Oh really?"

"Yes ma'am," I excitedly replied. "I talked about dinosaurs and how long they've been extinct."

"Oh…."

"Ummm Hmmm…and all the different species of dinosaurs that existed in this world."

"Interesting," replied Ms. Cox.

"Ma'am, did you know that alligators and crocodiles are just a few of the animals that survived after dinosaurs became extinct?"

"Don't forget about birds too, Nicholas," replied Ms. Cox.

"Oh yeaaaaa," I stated in amusement, "I forgot about that!"

"So, how was it being on TV?"

"At first, I was nervous, but after I read my notes, it was fun!"

"Notes?"

"Yes ma'am," I replied. "I had to write out notes to read on TV so I wouldn't forget what to say."

"Who helped with your notes?"

Smiling answering, I replied, "My mom...she's the best! She helps me with everything."

Ms. Cox takes a semi-long pause before saying, "Nicholas, go get your mother for me."

"Yes ma'am." I got up and rushed to the waiting area where my mother sat.

"Momma," I said. "Ms. Cox wants you to come in the office with us."

"Ok," she replies as she gets up from her chair.

We enter Ms. Cox's office and sit down in the two chairs

in front of her desk.

"Ms. Battle," she begins. "You're right. Nicholas is a gifted child. I would be honored to have him attend this school."

"Thank you so much ma'am," replied my mom.

"If he attends school here, you have to provide transportation to and from the school every day since he's not technically in our district."

"Ma'am that will be no problem."

"Do you have any relatives in this school district," asks Ms. Cox.

"No ma'am…why do you ask?"

"We need an address on file in this district to verify that you're zoned to attend school here."

My mother's facial expression suddenly looked like a person whose dog escaped and never came back. There was a definite somber look in her eyes and body language. She looks up at Ms. Cox and begins to speak.

"Ms. Cox, thank you for trying to make this work for us. Come on Nicholas, let's go."

"Ms. Battle," replied Ms. Cox. "My mother lives directly

across the street from the school. Maybe Nicholas can use her address as his home of record."

"You'd do that for us?"

"Indeed," she replied. "You do your part by getting him to school every day, and I'll do my part by making sure he has a district address on file. Deal?"

With a sudden joy of excitement, my mother replies, "Deal! Ms. Cox you will not regret this. We are so thankful!"

"Absolutely no problem. I look forward to having Nicholas on our campus!"

BATTLE'S BLUEPRINT

Never take "no" for an answer. Doing so would be submitting to failure, and failure is not an option. Always strive to do better.

My mother and I exit Ms. Cox's office and proceed out of the building to the car. She could not stop herself from smiling ear-to-ear. Initially, upon entering the school office a few hours earlier, I had no intention or desire to step foot on Southern Hill's schoolyard. It was my mother's excitement that compelled me to begin catching those same feelings. Seeing her proud of her only child drove me to reach heights of success I thought were unattainable. I realized failure was not an option in this new-found environment. Mom's sacrifice to put me in an unparalleled position assuring me of such privileges she never had the opportunity for, meant a lot to me. On the ride home from Southern Hills, I saw the joy on my mother's face. Her exuberant smile that day motivated me as she just accomplished a seemingly impossible deed. This is what drove me in continuing to work hard. Since this moment, my dedication is to continually keep that same smile on her face, as much as possible.

TRACK #3: START FROM SCRATCH

Artist: The Game

Album: The Documentary

The Compton MC touched my heart with this song.

"If I could start from scratch, I wouldn't change shit…"

These words could not have been truer to my life. Although my mother and I faced many hardships, those same struggles are what molded us to the strong unit we had become. I may have wished some things would have turned out differently, but my experiences are what makes me who I am.

I remember my first day of second grade like it was yesterday. Ms. Johnson was my teacher. She was firm, strict; but most importantly, fair. We probably had fifteen or so kids in the classroom, with me being the only minority. She pushed me hard…I mean harder than any other teacher I had previously; however, it only made me stronger. Ms. Johnson opened my pathways of thinking to a level I had yet to discover, and I appreciated that. That foundation prepared me for the remainder of my time at Southern Hills. I finished that school year with all "A's"…not a single B or worse.

For as well as things were going for me in school, life outside of school was difficult at times. Kids my age at the Village Square apartment complex that my mother and I lived at with my granny felt some type of way about me not attending school with them anymore. Some call it the "crab in a bucket" mentality. The meaning is if my peers could not have my advantage, neither should I. One peer of mine, JaVon, felt that way regarding me.

Back Up Off Me
Artist: Master P
Album: Ice Cream Man

After school every day, all the kids would meet in the open courtyard at Village Square. The complex was set up like a large square with a fifteen to twenty-foot gap in front to allow residents to attain entry into their apartments. Violence and unwanted foot traffic prompted the placement of a six-foot steel gate to alleviate crime. However, growing up the fence was non-existent.

Us kids would break the courtyard into three or four squares. One section might be playing football, the other section might be playing with a frisbee, while the other section might be playing around with no real purpose. I usually stuck to the football side of the courtyard with JaVon.

"Yo Nick," said JaVon. "We got next. Let's pick teams!"

"Cool...I got my team already, man."

"That's what's up...let me get mine right quick." JaVon scurries around the courtyard to assemble a team for the game.

"I'm good now bro," says JaVon. "Let's get it in!"

"Aight…bet!"

I ain't gonna lie. JaVon was a beast on the football field. He was a little bigger than the rest of us, but he wasn't as fast as me. I made sure I would always line up across from him when I played so that I could run past him for the possibility of getting a catch.

"Dang Nick…why you always gotta go against me," JaVon questioned.

"Man, just play bruh."

The quarterback yelled "Hike!" I ran past JaVon. The ball comes at me, but is too short. I come back for the ball, but JaVon runs straight into me.

"You can't run into me," I yelled. "That's a penalty man!"

"Man stop whining," screamed JaVon. "They don't teach you football at that little white school you go to?"

The other kids laughed at what JaVon said. I felt embarrassed because I had nothing to say. Yes, we played football and ran track during recess at Southern Hills, but me rambling on about that would just make me look weak. I ran back to the huddle. We call a play and I line up against JaVon again.

"Hey everybody," yells JaVon. "Nick thinks he's a white boy!"

The kids laugh again. I felt smaller than an ant, but I began to get angry as the laughter kept up.

"Say man," I insisted. "Chill!"

"Or what nigga?"

Any man challenged in such a manner before, knows not taking that challenge can change your life forever. I was already a smart kid, so coupling "smart" with "weak" would be a detrimental combination for me growing up in Village Square. I took a couple seconds to think before making my decision on what my next action would be.

"What's up then," I replied as I threw the first punch that was meant for JaVon's head but ended up hitting him on his shoulder.

The crowd of kids ran to us…not to stop the fight, but to form a circle around us and become spectators. JaVon swung back and hit me square in the chest. Remembering what my mother's brother, David, taught me, I ran and tackled JaVon to the ground.

Uncle David, better known as John Candy's famous character and movie title "Uncle Buck," would always tell me that the shorter the distance is between you and a person in a fight, the harder it is for them to get a big shot on you. As JaVon and I hit the ground, I sit on top of his chest and unleash five or six swings to him. As I'm swinging, the rage in me swelled. Picking on me for my new school, for being smart, or anything else—my fury poured out.

"Stooopp Nick!" yelled JaVon.

"I'm white though," I screamed back. "I should be easy right?"

"Nickkkk….stopppppp!"

I said no more words and kept swinging until another kid's parent came out and separated us. JaVon was crying and so was I. I had just got in a fight with a dude I thought was my boy. We played ball every day and ran through the courtyard like dogs off leashes. I quickly dried my eyes and JaVon went back inside his apartment.

As if nothing happened, the football game continued without hesitation.

"Who's taking JaVon's spot?" Someone yelled.

Another kid stepped up in his spot and the game went on. After a few plays, JaVon emerges back outside, this time accompanied by his older brother Reggie, who was either a freshman or sophomore in high school.

"Who touched my brother?!" He yelled.

No one said anything.

"Who the fuck touched my brother?! If y'all don't tell me, I'm fucking all y'all up!"

All the kids pointed at me. My heart sank to my stomach because I knew there was no getting out of this one. He walked over calmly to me before proceeding to whoop my ass.

"BOOM, BOOM," were the sounds of his fist as they hit me; once in the chest and the other in the stomach.

"Don't ever touch my muh' fucking brother again," he yelled.

I gained my composure and tried to take a swing on him. I missed and he punched me one more time in the stomach. I fell to the ground and curled up like a baby before he kicked me. He didn't say anything else. He just grabbed JaVon and they walked to their apartment.

I got up and dusted myself off. I wanted to cry but not in front of everyone. I walked back to my granny's apartment and walked into John-John's and my room. He was sitting on the edge of the bed playing Nintendo. I closed the door behind me and sat on the floor with my back pressed against the door. I was silent as a mouse. As a few moments passed by, John-John could sense something was wrong.

"You straight," he asked.

"Yea," I said in a semi-shakenly voice.

"Ok."

A few more moments pass by before I spoke up.

"John John…"

"Yea," he replied while playing his game.

I didn't know what to say so I just started crying. John-John paused his game and walked over to me.

"Nicholas, what's wrong?"

With tears running down my face and nose sniffling, I replied, "Someone beat me up!"

"Who!"

"JaVon's brother, Reggie!"

With a disgusted look on his face, John-John replies, "That nigga goes to my school!"

He storms out the house to go find Reggie but he was nowhere to be found. John-John came back into the house. I had cleaned my face up by now and was waiting for him to tell me he returned the ass whipping I got, back to Reggie.

"I didn't see him, but I know who he is. He's going to have to see me tomorrow!"

I nodded my head in reassurance that everything was going to be ok because I always knew that whatever John-John said he was going to do, he did. With him being just nine years older than me, he was more of an older brother to me than uncle. He potty-trained me, taught he how to talk to girls, showed me how to dress. If we're telling the truth, John-John had more to do with raising me than my own father ever did. He was my second superhero behind my PawPaw.

As the alarm went off the next morning, John-John woke me up.

"Nicholas," he said in a yawning voice, "Wake up and get ready for school."

I roll over and go back to sleep.

"Boyyy…you better get up before Renee gets you."

As if John-John's warning was a cue for my mother to rush into the room, she enters and begins to forcibly get me out of bed.

"Nicholas," she says, "Get up…time to go to school. You

know we can't be late!"

"Yes Ma'am."

"Come on…hurry up now."

I get up and get ready for school. My mom, John-John, and I pile into the big blue Ford Galaxy and make our way off to school. Since we were running a little late today, my mother drops me off first, and then John-John, who was currently on a straight mission to find Reggie.

As John-John enters Fair Park High School, he goes straight to the band room. He played trumpet, so him going there was not a shock; however, today his reasoning for going to the band room was different. Reggie was also in the high school band and John-John went to check his chin.

"John-John, what up bro," says J.J., one of John-John's close friends.

"Not today J.J.," he replied. "Where's Reggie at?"

"That fool somewhere in the back."

"Bet that," says John-John as he storms to the back of the band hall.

"Yo Reggie…where you at nigga," yells John-John.

With a puzzled look on his face, Reggie replies, "What's

good bro…what's wrong?"

"Please tell me my nephew got this wrong, bro…."

"What's happening?"

"You hit a lil' kid yesterday bro?"

"That was your neph…...?"

Before Reggie could finish his statement, John-John knew exactly what the answer was based on his facial expression. He laid a two-punch combo to Reggie's face before slamming him into a locker in the band hall. John-John's persistent pressure levied on Reggie caught him off guard. He tried to fight back, but it was too little, too late. A couple of band members separated, or rather peeled John-John off Reggie.

Wiping the streaming blood from his nose, Reggie pleads, "John-John…I didn't know that was your family…"

"Nigga, now you know. And if you ever look at my nephew again, I'll beat yo ass again," rambled John-John. "Hoe ass nigga beating up on a second grader…you a bitch!"

John-John walked out the band hall and to his first class. Reggie posed no fear to him, as he realized that Reggie was a coward who was bold enough to step up to a seven-year old, but too scared to bring that same energy at a sixteen-year old peer.

Reggie looked dumbfounded and defeated. He had no words to say. The same embarrassment I felt playing football with JaVon a day earlier, transferred squarely onto Reggie. I'm pretty sure Reggie must remember that ass whooping to this day…not because he got beat up, but because of the reasoning behind it.

When I got home later that afternoon, I looked at John-John and he nodded. His unsaid words spoke volumes to me. Super Hero #2 came to my rescue, and I felt comfort and pleasure in that.

BATTLE'S BLUEPRINT
Stay straight with your Day-ones. You cannot bend what does not fold.

When I look back at the entire situation with JaVon, I understand the reason for our altercation. JaVon and I had the same card dealer in life. We both had single mothers trying to raise young black boys into men. With my mother making an asserted effort to send me to a better school, it placed me on a better platform to achieve success more so than JaVon; even though we came from the same neighborhood. Since we were essentially "cut from the same cloth," and my potential was now greater than his, at least from an educational standpoint, JaVon may have begun to look down on me as if I was outgrowing "us."

My success of getting the opportunity to have access to a better school manifested raw emotion to jealousy and envy, which later transpired to violence. Our feud was not due to me having the opportunity to better myself. It was just JaVon's frustration of not having that same opportunity at that moment.

BATTLE'S BLUEPRINT
Never make real decisions based on emotions.

In hindsight, it's not JaVon's fault of why he felt that way. It's a stigma that our black culture had placed on us for multiple generations to keep us in as segregated an environment as possible. JaVon's attempt to reduce my confidence in achieving something greater in life than what we were purvey to daily is justifiable. It's a simple effort to assure him that if he could have the opportunity to become successful and leave our environment, there might be an opportunity waiting for him in the limited spots available to people who "look like him." JaVon's thought patterns of opportunities seized by someone he does not know is justifiable because their story is unknown to him. If I received that opportunity, it's quite the opposite. When JaVon looks at me, it's essentially him looking in the mirror. I understand…

This Can't Be Life
Artist: Jay-Z (Ft Beanie Sigel and Scarface)
Album: Dynasty – Roc La Familia -

The crack epidemic hit America in the mid-1980s and has continued to sustain itself until today. Staying between the two of my grandmother's houses allowed me to see how powerful the drug was up-and-close. From our Motown user, Leon, to other users across each neighborhood, it became an everyday event to see these "zombie" individuals wade through their normal lives. As a resident surrounded by it, you become numb to seeing these individuals. This epidemic made itself an unwanted but integral part of our lives. Living in our neighborhoods meant no one went unaffected, as numerous family members became addicted to the drug.

My mom's younger brother, Bryant, is one of the smartest individuals I know. He was a master musician and played the trumpet in high school. Anyone who has ever heard him play raves about his talent. His high school band director, Mr. White, told my granny that he was one of the best, if not the best, trumpet player he ever instructed. Bryant played music by ear. He could read music; however, his musical flair outpaced the music sheet. He literally moved to the sound of his own music.

When he graduated high school, he received a band scholarship to play at Texas Southern University. When his educational aspirations didn't come to fruition, he would later join the Navy and serve six years before an honorable discharge and returning home.

In my eyes, my Uncle Bryant is the epitome of talent. Rumor has it that he would disassemble appliances as a youth, only to piss my granny off, before reassembling them to a perfect configuration. As a youth, the talent he had intrigued me.   I wanted to build things. I wanted to take machines apart. I wanted to play instruments. All that stemmed from Bryant. That's my dude…even to this day.

For as talented as Bryant was, he was not shielded from the horrors of the crack epidemic. I don't know when he started using the narcotic; however, I watched as my talented uncle gradually became a shell of himself. No longer was he the enthusiastic and playful uncle that I had become accustomed to and grown up with. He was now a guy that our family did not understand…a guy that started to remind us of the people we had become numb to within our environment.

My grandma Vergie was the sweetest soul you'd ever meet. She was a mother of eight and always enjoyed a full-house and large gathering, as evident by the number of children and grandchildren that stayed with her daily. On some occasions, you'd have granny, my mother, John-John, Bryant, my cousin BC, and myself under one roof. The love of family outweighed the lack of space in granny's eyes. Her family was with her, and that's all that mattered.

As stated previously, my granny suffered a stroke a few years earlier and she couldn't "police" the house like once before. Bryant was the oldest male in the apartment, so naturally, he was the man of the house. Responsibilities obviously fell to Bryant, as exemption was not an option.

My granny had a few errands to run one Saturday afternoon, so we all piled into the car to do as she asked. It was an all-day excursion. We started out at the mall, where my granny went to JCPenney and Dillard's to shop around.

After her stroke, my granny needed a cane to assist her walk, but that never stopped her from accomplishing what she wanted to do. We might have walked that mall all of three hours, but we didn't complain because it's what, granny, or as my cousin BC called her, "Big Momma," wanted.

"Big Momma," says BC in her sassy voice. "It's time to eat."

"BC," replied my granny in matter of fact tone. "We'll eat when we leave here."

"Yes ma'am."

We stroll through the mall for another twenty minutes before going to the car. Big Momma gets into the passenger seat after me, BC, and John-John load into the back seat. My mother gets into the driver seat and starts the car.

"What do y'all want to eat," asks Big Momma.

With a quick reply, John-John says, "Burger King!" He loved their double whopper with cheese, bacon, and a side of BBQ sauce to later throw on the burger for that extra flavor. To this day, that's the only way I eat my whoppers.

"Everybody good with that," says Big Momma.

A collective, "yes," resounded in the car and we began our way to Burger King. We go through the drive-thru and pick up our meals.

"Renee," says Big Momma. "Check the bag and make sure they cut my whopper in half like I asked."

"It's cut momma."

"Good," she replies. "Now drive on down to Southern Maid and get a dozen donuts."

BC's eyes lit up at the sound of Southern Maid Donuts. This sweet spot was her absolute favorite place to go after 4pm because donuts came hot and fresh off the machine. Since it was nearly 6pm, it was the perfect time to get the tasty treats. We pull up to the donut shop and BC and I hop out the car and go in the store.

"Dozen glazed," requested BC to the cashier. "Nicholas, you want something else?"

"Ummm…a red Jungle Juice."

"And get my cousin a red Jungle Juice too."

The cashier reaches behind herself and grabs a jungle juice and hands it to me.

"Thank you."

"You're welcome," she replied. "Dozen donuts up!"

BC walks to the counter and grabs her donuts. "Thank ya."

We leave the store and head back to the car. By now, everyone has finished their Burger King and began to devour the donuts. What a time to be alive!

"Renee," says Big Momma. "Stop by County Market so we can pick up a few things for me to cook tomorrow evening."

"Yes ma'am," replies my mom as we head to the grocery store. As we arrive and park, Big Momma hands my mom fifteen dollars.

"Renee, I need a package of neck bones and beans. I'll soak them tonight a cook them all day tomorrow."

"Ok Momma," replies my mom as she exits the car to retrieve the items. After a short period of time, my mom comes back to the car with everything Big Momma asked for.

It's around 7:30pm now and dark. We head back to Big Momma's apartment and walk up to the door. As John-John unlocks the door to go into the house, he turns the living room light on.

"John-John," says Big Momma. "Why in the hell did you leave this house looking like this?"

"Momma, I cleaned the living room before I left. I swear..."

"So, I guess a ghost missed up all this stuff in front of this window?"

With an uneasy tone in my mother's voice, she interjects, "Momma, where's the VCR?"

"Where it's supposed to be! Under my TV!"

"Momma," she replies. "It ain't there..."

With a sigh under her breath, Big Momma replies, "Bryant..."

John-John looks at the window. It's unlocked. He and I go outside the apartment to see the screen. Someone had sloppily placed it back on the window.

"This nigga unlocked the window before we all left and came back to get the damn VCR," John-John said to himself. "Nicholas, go inside."

I go back into the house and hear my mother on the phone talking to my Uncle David.

"Yea, David," she says. "The VCR is gone!"

Through the muffled phone speaker, I could hear David mutter, "I'm on my way over!"

As my mom hangs up the phone, she sits down on the living room couch in disbelief. Big Momma sat in her lazy-boy chair with a semi angry, yet somber glare on her face. On one hand, she was furious that her son had stolen from her. On the other hand, she was sad that her son felt like he had to steal from her. Big Momma was in a state of confusion and just did not know how to handle it.

What seemed like just moments after their phone call, my mother was opening the door for my Uncle David to come in the apartment.

"Where is he," says Uncle David.

"David…I don't know," replies Big Momma. Her hope was that Bryant doesn't show up for fear of an altercation between her two sons; however, he must have known somebody was thinking of him because Bryant entered the house…as if nothing had happened.

"What's up y'all?"

David, with a puzzled look on his face responds, "What do you mean what's up?"

"What's wrong with you?"

"Bryant, don't act like you don't know. I know you took momma's VCR. Where the hell is it?"

With an uneasy look on his face, Bryant points his head down, knowing that he's caught red-handed.

"Say something!" David screamed.

Bryant still uttered no words.

For fear of knowing something was about to happen, Big Momma got up and went to her room. I left and went to my bedroom also. A loud commotion occurred in the living room. There was a bunch of yelling, mostly from Uncle David. I didn't want to know what he did to Bryant because I loved both of my uncles so much. I guess the only images I wanted of my uncles was that of a unified force.

I held my hands over my eyes while sitting Indian style on the floor, waiting for everything to end. After a few moments, my Uncle David called for Big Momma to come back into the room. Mentally, I assessed that as the cue for me to come back into the living room also.

As I entered the living room, Bryant was sitting on the

couch with his head down. Big Momma had taken her normal spot in her Lazy Boy chair. Everyone else was standing.

"Bryant," said Uncle David. "You have something you wanna tell momma?"

"Momma," he replies. "It won't happen again. I promise…I'm tryin' to change."

"I know Bryant…I know…"

I'm Ready
Artist: The Diplomats
Album: Diplomatic Immunity

At the end of my second-grade school year, my mother was able to secure her own apartment. We moved to a newer complex called Southside Villas across the Jewella Bridge in Shreveport. It was a two-bedroom, one-bathroom apartment with brown carpet throughout. There was a decent sized living room and smaller dining room as you first walked in the apartment. A small kitchen was off the dining room. In front of the living room was a hallway that led to my room on the left-hand side of the hallway, while the bathroom and my mom's bedroom was on the right. The hallway dead-ended to a small linen closet. My mother was also able to get her first car. It was a 1982 two-door champagne colored Honda Accord hatchback. I can't even lie, when we got our own spot and car, I felt like we made it. My mom was so happy and proud to provide for me. I was happy for her because I knew everything she went through to get us where we needed to be in life.

My mom bust her ass every day, working as a secretary, to provide the furniture in the house. We were able to get a glass dining room table that my mother made me eat at every night. We had a beautiful solid-wood television cabinet and a nice couch. I had bunkbeds, a dresser, and a small TV on a stand in my room. My mom had a full-size bed against the back wall of her room, a dresser on the right-hand side, and a chest on the front wall with a TV on top of it. My mom created the perfect environment for us to succeed…at least for now. We were happy. We had each other, and that's all we needed.

Just like Big Momma, my mom enjoyed having family around…all the time. It was common for us to have someone at our apartment. Whether it was BC and her mother, Aunt Linda, visiting us, or my mom's best friend and my cousin Jay's mom, Daphne coming by; we always had visitors and a bunch of fun.

Some of my fondest memories growing up were having my cousin BC take me to the arcade in the South Park Mall, which was right across the street from our apartment. I always loved playing games, but with my mother's limited funds, I was never able to play as many games as I would like; however, BC would always look out for me.

"Excuse me," BC called over to the arcade worker.

"Yes…are there any problems with the games?"

"Yes, there is," she replied in her now tuned-up flirtatious voice. "My cousin ran out of money, so he needs some more games."

"Well ma'am…"

Cutting off the worker from finishing his sentence, BC says, "You're cute…what's your name?"

"Uhhhhh…Ronny," he replies in a bashful way.

"Well Ronny, like I said…my cousin needs some more games."

Ronny glanced at me and asked, "Hey lil' man, what

game do you want to play?"

"Streets of Rage," I replied.

Ronny walked over to the game and inserts his universal key into the machine.

"Press start lil' man, you got two free games on there."

"Thank you," I replied in amusement.

After my game had ended, BC and I left the mall to go back to our apartment. We hop in her red Hyundai Excel coupe.

"You see," she said laughing. "You're gonna get to play all them games for free!" As she continues to chuckle, she goes on to say, "Shiiiittttt…I'm gonna get him to get us some Southern Maid too!"

I bust out laughing too. We started driving back home and, in that moment, I realized BC was ride-or-die for me. Ever since I was a baby and had to pronounce her name as "Bing-Bing" because I couldn't say "BC." It wasn't just a free video game from some dude named Ronny, rather, it was because she took the time to assure, I didn't want for anything. Come Hell or high-water, she was going to make sure I was good.

We get back to the apartment and walk inside laughing

and giggling about what had just happened.

"What y'all so loud for," said my mom, as she's watching TV. Star Trek being on meant no one was to disturb her while watching it.

At the commercial break, I begin to tell my mom about our day. "Momma, BC got me some free games at the arcade!"

"That's sweet. Did you thank BC for the games?"

"Don't thank me," said BC. "Thank Ronny!"

BC and I both began to laugh hysterically while my mother looked at us like we were crazy.

"Who's Ronny," she replied.

"My couusssssinnn wanted to play some video games," BC said with her hand on her hip and eyes rolled. "He ran out of tokens, so I got the arcade manager to get him some free ones."

BC glances at me and says, "And you had fun too...didn't you Nicholas!"

"Yep!"

"See," replied my mom with a smiling gesture. "That's why I can't send my baby anywhere with you!"

"What you mean, Renee," said BC. "You need to check

your baaabbbyyy. He pimped me for the free tokens!"

The three of us just bust out in laughter. My mother had a laugh so hard, that it brought the, "Oh, Lawd," phrase out of her. I had tears streaming from my eyes over how hard I laughed.

Just when we thought it couldn't get any funnier, BC goes on to say, "Girl, I done already told him that if you meet a girl just like your cousin Bing-Bing, you run yo ass in the complete opposite direction!"

With Mom literally sprawled out on the couch laughing uncontrollably, someone knocked at the door.

"Who is it," my mom says while trying to subdue her laughter.

"Bryant."

My mom opens the door to let my uncle in. "I heard y'all all the way outside. What the hell are y'all laughing so hard about?"

Still laughing, my mother said, "Your niece!"

He laughs before making an announcement. "So, I got some good news y'all!"

"What you got Bryant," replies my mom.

"I got a job close around here."

We all cheer, in our crazy and joking way. My mother expressed how proud she was of my uncle and the direction he was heading.

"Thanks Renee," says Bryant hesitantly. "But…I need to ask you a favor…"

"Ummmm hmmmmm…."

"Can I stay here for a little while…just until I get everything rolling right?"

Without hesitation, my mother replied, "Yea, you can stay…as long as you're fine with this couch."

"Come on Renee," he replied with laughter and an apparent sigh of relief. "You know I ain't trippin' on that!"

The smile on her face at that moment was undeniable because, although we were away from Big Momma's apartment and on our own, the vibes we had were still one in the same. The love for my family was second-to-none and I was glad to have a scaled-down resemblance of the unity we always had at Big Momma's.

Although my uncle had previously had a problem with addiction, it all seemed like a distant memory. We were family, and no matter what, family stuck together to help us get through troubling times. This situation was no different.

U Don't Got a Clue
Artist: Nipsey Hussle
Album: The Marathon

Growing up, I only knew one of my grandfathers. My dad's father, my PawPaw, was one of the most monumental figures in my life. For that reason, as a youth, I never understood the lack of involvement from my mother's father. I can recall meeting him only once in my lifetime, and that recollection is not based off physical memory. I can attest to this moment only because I saw an old Polaroid photo of me sitting in his lap as a child. I was maybe three or four years old based on my size in the picture.

As I grew older, I became more inquisitive about my grandfather. I knew that he was only my mom and Uncle Bryant's father; however, I had more questions. What did his voice sound like? How tall was he? What did his house look like? What kind of car did he drive?

Sometimes I would create an imaginary façade of my inquiries. One day, I might impersonate him by using a deep voice…but then I figured he couldn't be too tall because my mom and Uncle Bryant were not that tall. So, I would self-correct myself by adjusting my voice to mimic Bryant's. Hell, it had to be similar since he was his father.

Eventually, my mom would tell me that my grandfather struggled with alcohol addiction.   She would tell me the stories of her youth…having to put him to bed after a long drunken night. She would have to take his shoes off, lay him down, and place him on his side in case he vomited.

I remember being in complete shock and awe hearing my mom's story about my grandfather. I could not understand why he wasn't my other superhero, just as my PawPaw was. Living through the reality that all grandfathers possessed greatness was untrue, altered my vision of what a superhero was.

With my Uncle Bryant now staying with us, I felt as though I always had a piece of my grandfather with me. Judging from the photo I had, Bryant was a near exact replica of him. I never felt the need to ask him about his father because I had him…Bryant.

I studied Bryant's mannerisms and tried to emulate them, thinking maybe this could make me closer to someone

I had no relationship with. I mimicked hand gestures, eating habits, laughter, and just about anything else to unify my grandfather and I in some fashion. That was the only way I thought I could get an absolute connection to him.

The years of alcohol abuse had finally taken a toll on my grandfather. My mother received a call from one of our cousins in Dallas, Texas regarding his declining health. The call revealed a diagnosis of terminal liver cancer. After she hung up from the phone call, my mom called us all into the living room.

"Bryant," she said. "Daddy's sick with liver cancer."

"Naw Renee!"

"They're saying he doesn't have much time to live, so I'm going to head up to Dallas tomorrow to see him. You wanna come with me?"

"I gotta work…but how long do you think you'll be up there," he replied.

"A couple days."

"I'll catch the bus down there tomorrow when I get off and go see him. Then I'll just drive back to Shreveport with you when it's time to leave."

"Ok."

Part of me was sad because my grandfather was in the late stages of losing his life. Part of me was semi-anxious to see him, no matter if he was in a hospital bed or not. I just wanted to see him, at least, at a minimum, to see a piece of me in him.

The next morning, my mom and I load into her Honda Accord and make our way down to Dallas. It was a three-hour drive; however, the tone in the car was a tad melancholy. I can't imagine what my mom was thinking as she drove to the hospital. She was literally driving to visit and possibly say her last words to her father. I had no words to console my mom. I just didn't know what to do.

The trip seemed longer than it was because of the reasoning behind us traveling, but we finally arrived at the hospital. We park the car and walk into the hospital lobby.

"Ma'am," stated the receptionist. "How may I help you?"

"I need the room number for Mr. Billy Ray Battle, please."

"Are you family?"

"Yes, I'm his daughter."

"Room 217, ma'am."

"Thank you," replied my mom as we walked towards the elevator. I press the number two and the elevator rises a floor. 'Ding,' rang the elevator bell before its doors opened.

We walk down the hallway until we see the room number '217' to the left of the door. My mom stops me first by putting her hands on my shoulder. She enters the room, to see my grandfather resting in his hospital bed. She motions me to come in. I walk forward and stand next to my mom as I finally get to see my grandfather. His hair was grey and balding with the same hair pattern as my Uncle Bryant. In fact, he looked like a carbon copy of Bryant, just an older version. He was a smaller-figured guy and not tall at all. He was maybe 5 feet 6 inches…7 inches if we're stretching it. We sat by his bed for a few hours before we left. We waited on Bryant, but he didn't make it in yet. We thought that maybe the Greyhound bus was running later than expected.

The next morning, we arrived back at the hospital. We still haven't heard from Bryant, so my mother begins to get a little worried about his whereabouts. She calls our apartment phone line, with no answer. She tries again…still no answer. She waits around the hospital until the latest moment possible before we had to leave. My mom walks back into my grandfather's hospital room and kisses him on the forehead as he rests. I place my hand on his shin as I look up to him in the bed. I walk out of the room while my mother has a silent, alone moment with him to possibly pay her final respects. After a moment, we head to our car to begin our trek back to Shreveport.

"Where in the hell is Bryant," my mom asks herself while merging onto Dallas' I-20 traffic.

My mom's voice seemed unsure and uneasy of what she felt was the reason for Bryant's absence in Dallas. I could see the thoughts that were racing through her head. Was something wrong with Bryant? Did we mistakenly give him the wrong hospital name? Did his Greyhound bus break down? We had no answer to what could be the problem. The only thing we could do is drive home and pray for the best.

The three-hour drive home seemed like a blur. My mom let that Honda's engine breath down Highway I-20. We pass Terrell, Texas...then Tyler, Texas...through Longview, Texas...and then Marshall, Texas. Thirty minutes later, we reach the Louisiana border and then take the Jewella exit. We cross the bridge and then continue down Jewella until we stop at the traffic light in front of the Blockbuster Video Store next to our apartment complex. The light turns green and we make an immediate right turn before making a sharp left into the complex.

My mom parks in front of our apartment door, and we both exit the vehicle and go to our front door. My mom inserts the key into the lock, while simultaneously opening the door. Our next view was a complete shock. The living room and dining room were completely empty. The couch, the solid wood TV wall unit accompanied with our TV, and the dining room table were all gone. My mom paces to the bedrooms to see the exact same visual. Everything was gone.

My mom walks back to the living room in as defeated of a manner as I have ever seen her. She tilts her head down before ultimately falling to her knees with her head touching the ground. Everything she worked for was now gone except for a portrait hanging in the hallway of she and I. If God was sending us a message, it must have been that even if you have nothing, you still have each other. No matter what the meaning was, the circumstance was crushing.

Oddly enough, during our brief time of grief, someone knocked on our door. My mom answers it to the surprise of our neighbor from the upstairs apartment, Ms. Mun.

"Girl, I'm mad at you," she said. "How you gonna just up and decide to move out and not tell nobody?"

With a confused look on her face, my mom replies, "What?"

"Girl stop playing," she jokingly said. "Bryant told me y'all were moving. He and his friend loaded all the furniture on the U-Haul already. Girl, he's a hell-of-a packer, for real. That boy even wrapped the frozen meats in bed sheets. I was like damnnnn!"

My mom walks to the kitchen to see whether what Ms. Mun was telling her was true. She opened the freezer door, and just as Ms. Mun stated, it was empty. The look on my mom's face went from defeated to disgusted. She walked back into the empty living room.

"Ms. Mun," my mom said. "We aren't leaving or moving anywhere. Bryant just took all our shit!"

"What you mean?"

With her hands grabbing the crown of her head, she looks up and says in a loud voice, "Girl, he robbed us!" Pronouncing every syllable, she reiterates her original statement, "He really just took e-ve-ry-thing."

With a shocked looked on her face, Ms. Mun expresses her apologies for the situation. "Billie, if I would have known, I…."

"Don't hold this against yourself," interjects my mom. "You didn't know, but if you did, I know you would have stopped it."

"Girl, do you need anything…a place to stay tonight…anything?"

With an embarrassed look on her face, my mother replies that we'll be ok. Ms. Mun left our apartment and went back to hers. My mother calls her brother David to inform him of the situation. She and I grabbed a few clothes, got back in our car, and head over to his house for a few nights before my mom wraps her head around what just occurred.

For as far as we came as a two-person unit, my mom and I were back at ground zero. But no matter the grave situation that had just occurred, we'd strive through…just as always. We're fighters and honestly, there's no better fighter than Billie Renee. As hurtful as this instance has been, it was just a minor setback for a major comeback.

BATTLE'S BLUEPRINT
Tough times don't last…tough people do.

TRACK #4: FATHER'S DAY

Artist: Mac

Album: World War III

Mac is, without a doubt, the most lyrical MC Louisiana has ever produced.

The hook in this song screams to me.

"Daddy do you love me…and if so, why you wasn't there to hug me and watch me grow?"

A young black male growing up without a father usually leads to a dark path, unless you had a mother like mine.

Lil' Ghetto Boy
Artist: Dr. Dre Feat Snoop Dogg and Daz
Album: The Chronic

The summer leading into my third-grade year was rough. As a young black male growing up with a single mother, I had a lot of questions concerning the state of black men in this country. I needed direct answers from another black man, preferably my father.

Just a few months earlier, on March 3, 1991, the Rodney King incident occurred. I was at my PawPaw and grandmother's house when the video of Mr. King's traffic stop surfaced. I was in shock and awe at what I had just seen. Four police officers beat him with batons more than 50 times while another 5 or so officers stood by and observed the "show." My PawPaw usually worked nights; however, tonight he was off work.

Just a year earlier, I witnessed my first murder. I grew up in an area where waking up to gunshots in the middle of the night was not unusual. Drug and alcohol abusers were a common thing within the neighborhoods I grew up in.

Relatives and close friends grew up to become drug pushers and dealers. For all that I had seen throughout my short-lived life, this incident deeply affected me because Rodney King was 25 years old; the exact same age as my Uncle Rodney. Rodney "King" could have easily been Rodney "Brown."

Police brutality was something that blacks have experienced our entire lives; however, this incident was on a whole other level. Growing up you saw images and videos of the "past" segregated south. They revealed disturbing pictures and videos of blacks being severely mistreated. High pressure fire hoses took people off their feet, rabid police dogs leapt after them. Adding insult to injury, police officers beat many in plain sight. Our country's desegregation was legal, however, the mentality of some never accepted any notions of an integrated America.

My grandmother sat motionless in her recliner in the den, while my PawPaw and I sat on the couch.

"Earl," said my grandmother. "This shit ain't right!"

"Yea...I know," replied PawPaw. "I'm going to call Honey Bunch to check up on her in a minute."

Honey Bunch was PawPaw's mother, who lived in

South Central Los Angeles during that time. She had my PawPaw when she was fifteen or sixteen years old. She left him with his father's family in Shreveport, as she relocated to Los Angeles in the late 1940s.

"Yea Earl," replied grandma. "Please do. Check on her to make sure she's alright."

"PawPaw," I said. "Why are they beating that man like that? Couldn't they just get on his back and put handcuffs on him?"

"Shotgun," PawPaw says in a comforting voice. "Sometimes evil people do evil things. They don't care about doing what's right…they only care about doing what they want."

"But, it ain't right PawPaw. I mean, they keep playing it over and over PawPaw…and each time I see it, I keep thinking there must be something he keeps doing for them to keep beating him. But, he ain't doing nothing PawPaw. They just keep beating him."

My PawPaw breathes a huge sigh of disbelief. He was at a loss for words.

"Shotgun," he says. "I just don't know…I just don't know."

I stayed at my grandparent's house that night. We kept switching the television between different news channels to see if there were any new updates concerning Rodney King. I usually had to be in bed by 9PM; however, PawPaw let me stay up until almost midnight as we watched the news coverage, even though I had school in the morning. I dozed off on the couch before heading into my room to go to sleep. Waking up would be rough in the morning, but not as rough as the images I had seen the night before.

The following morning, I got up and got ready for school. PawPaw drove me to Southern Hills that day. School went on as normal up until lunch before we formed into our single-file line to head to the cafeteria. We grab our trays and sit down at our table to eat as I hear a muffled conversation at the table behind me.

"Did you see the video of the cops beating up that dude last night," said an unfamiliar voice.

"Yea," replied another. "My daddy said that he deserved it."

"Yep…mine too," said the first voice. "My momma said that if he would have just stopped moving, they would have stopped beating him. But…that's what a nigger gets."

In pure disgust, I turned around to the voices directly behind me. I'll never forget what the kid who made that last statement looked like. He was a white kid with a short brown hair cut, shaped like a "bowl" around his head. He had brown eyes and a couple moles on his right cheek. My eyes locked onto his. Now fully exposed as a purveyor of racist rhetoric, I could literally feel his heart drop to his stomach.

The face behind the voice was scared and I was mad, but neither of us knew what to say to each other. I continued to glare at him, as if we were having a stare-down contest. The kid nodded his head down in embarrassment, knowing that he said something he knew was not right; however, he was only repeating what he learned at home.

BATTLE'S BLUEPRINT

Do not conform to ignorance. Educate yourself on subjects you are unfamiliar with and continue to build your knowledge base by acquiring more information on subjects you are familiar with.

It wasn't the fact that we disagreed on whether Rodney King deserved the senseless beating he received, it was the notion that he had to demean Mr. King by using derogatory language to describe him, suggesting that Rodney King was beneath him. If this kid felt this way about Rodney King, what did he think of me? Obviously, in his eyes, I was on the same playing field as Mr. King…just another nigger.

As if on cue, Mrs. Johnson directs my class to prepare to leave the cafeteria to head back to the classroom. A huge sigh of relief came over the kid's face. My class lined up against the lunchroom wall and walked out. I would see the kid from time-to-time at school, either on the playground at recess or when our classes passed each other on the outside hallways in route to another room. He would always continue to avoid me, no matter the situation. Hopefully, the embarrassment he felt while facing me discouraged him from other instances as the one he had with me…just hopefully.

The Rodney King incident was a constant reminder to my mom of the dangers black men had to encounter throughout this crazy world. I was eight years old and she was only twenty-six. My dad wasn't a constant presence in my life, so I couldn't turn to him for guidance with issues like this. My Uncle Bryant was fresh off robbing us blind, and my Uncle John-John was a seventeen-year-old high school student that was still a kid himself.

Although my mom was my "mom," we essentially grew up together. She was a great parent, mainly through a lot of on-the-job training. To instill principles and beliefs in me that needed a father's conversation, she would explain what she thought was correct and then reinforce that conversation with a visual representation. Her aim was to mentally stimulate my thinking and spark an inner-conversation within myself.

A few months after Rodney King's beating, a commercial aired for a movie that looked like it was set in the center of Motown or Queensborough.

"Momma," I said. "I want to see that!"

"Boy, that movie is rated R," she replied.

"But momma...," I said as the commercial ended.

My momma read the title of the movie. "Boyz N Da Hood," she said internally. She looked at the TV screen and then looked at me. She thought about it for a few minutes.

"Nicholas, when does that movie come out?"

"Tomorrow."

"Ok," mom replied. "Tomorrow...we're going to the movies."

"Really?!" I asked in excitement.

"Yes…really," replied mom as she told me to go to bed as it was getting late.

I was so excited to see this movie because, for one, the title was an exact copy of one of N.W.A.'s most popular songs, plus Ice Cube was one of John-John's favorite rappers at that time. I went to sleep in a hurry, anticipating going out with my mom tomorrow night for the movie. Tomorrow couldn't get here any sooner.

It was Saturday night. The movie was set to start in about an hour. As we get ready to leave the house, my mom yells some marching orders to me.

"Nicholas," she said. "Go and get my black purse out the closet."

"The big one?"

"Yea…that one."

I go to my mom's closet to get her purse. As I grab the purse, I realize how "big" of a purse this was.

"Momma…why do you gotta have this purse," I said. "It's huge."

"Do you wanna eat at the movies," she says sarcastically.

"Yep!"

"Well, hush then!"

We leave the house and stop by the gas station on our way to the movie theater. We go inside and go straight to the candy aisle.

"Hot tamales momma, and…" I began to say.

"Milk duds and Bit-O-Honey," replied momma.

"What else momma?"

"What kind of coke do you want?"

"Hmmm…peach Faygo."

"Ok," my mom replied as we headed towards the coolers in the back of the store. She picked up a canned peach Faygo and another canned Coca-Cola. She pays for it and we head out the gas station to go see the movie.

As we enter the movie theater, we head straight to the room where our movie was. It was a crowded house already, as the movie was about to start in just a few minutes. We found two seats midway from the bottom on the right-hand side of the theater.

I look around the theater and recognized that everyone there looked just like me, apart from a couple of white faces in the audience. I remember the commercials I had seen the past few weeks leading up to the movie debut. Much of the press stated that this was a "must-see" movie. Shit, even Roger Ebert gave the movie his highest reward, a 4-star rating.

The lights begin to dim and the movie commercials begin to play. I tap my mom on the leg. She turns towards me.

"Momma," I whispered. "Can I have my Faygo?"

"Not now…wait until after the usher does his aisle walk-through and the movie starts,' she replies with an even more silent whisper.

"Ok."

As on cue, the movie theater employee walked down the aisles in the theater to make sure no one had snuck in any food or drinks. As the usher begins to turn down our aisle, my mom leans over to me.

"Keep your head forward," she whispered. "Don't pay him any attention."

"Ok momma."

The usher walked down the aisle and glances through each row. I kept my head straight and looking at the screen, just as momma told me. I probably *over* acted, as my neck was literally stiff like a manikin. The usher turned around to walk back up the aisle before leaving the theater.

The opening scene begins with a young character named "Tre" who was of similar age as me. With my eyes set upon the screen, I hear a coke can opening. I look to my right as my mom taps my knee and hands me my peach Faygo.

"Momma," I said. "What about my Hot Tamales?"

She opens the box from the top and hands the candy to me.

"Here," replies mom.

I drank my Faygo and ate my Hot Tamales as I watched the movie. Tre, Doughboy, and Ricky were just like my family members. I could relate to everything that went on in the movie. I had no trouble paying attention.

I was Tre, and ironically, my mom was Tre's father, Furious Styles. She was smart...she was a disciplinarian...she laid down the rules and expected me to follow them without question. She kept me in sports and different activities to assure that I wouldn't have the time to chase trouble in the streets of Shreveport.

Although she couldn't see everything I was doing, the foundation my mom set for me was impenetrable. When the lures of gangs and drugs approached me at an early age, the benchmark set by my mom was of a higher caliber than what either of those two vices could provide. She was strong-willed and determined to set the perfect example, as both my mother and father.

In a scene towards the end of the movie where Doughboy attempts to get revenge for his brother's untimely demise, the movie theater became totally silent. Doughboy pulled up to the burger joint in his impala and turned the headlights off.

"Awww shit," said a voice in front of me.

Doughboy drives his car towards the guys who murdered his brother. His friend pulls out the Ak-47 and props himself up in the car. He lets off the first round of bullets.

"Hell yea…get that nigga," shouted another voice in the theater.

"Buss his ass," yelled another.

After the drive-by happened, Doughboy gets out the car and walks up to one of the guys. Noticing he was still alive, he kicks the man, shoots him, and kills him before fleeing.

The crowd erupted and began to clap after Doughboy got revenge. Wanting to feel inclusive and not detached from everyone else in the theater, I too began to clap before my mom grabbed my hands to silence my cheer.

"Nicholas," my mom said. "Never applaud a man taking another man's life…especially a black man taking the life of another black man."

"Yes ma'am," I replied as we watched the movie until its end. As the credits begin to roll and we exit the theater, I reflected on the movie and what my mom said during Doughboy's revenge scene. As we get into the car and drive home, my mom and I discuss the movie.

"What did you think about the movie, Nicholas?"

"I liked it momma. It was so real."

"Real," she asked. "What do you mean?"

"Well, I feel like South Central was like Motown…or Queensborough."

"How so?"

"It's like…when Tre's girlfriend was at home doing her school work and she heard gunshots…"

"Umm hmmm," says my mom.

"It reminded me of when I'm at my grandma and PawPaw's house. Even the sound of the gunshots was the same," as I described the sounds that an Ak-47 makes.

"Besides that, what did you learn?"

"I learned that when you do bad things to others, like the guy who killed Ricky…then bad things will happen to you."

"So, what about Ricky's brother," my mom asks. "He did something bad also."

"Yea, and he was killed also," I said as the wheels began to turn in my head.

"Momma," I asked. "So, do the bad things just never stop ending? I mean, if the guy who killed Ricky gets killed by Doughboy…then Doughboy gets killed after that…then the person who killed Doughboy will probably die too, right?"

"They don't have to die," replies my mom. "All the killing can end if we choose to stop it."

"I get it momma. So, it's like you always tell me. Sometimes you must be the bigger man, right?"

"Exactly," my mom replies. "The strongest person is always the one who doesn't do something based on their emotions. It's easy to do something and then blame it on 'rage,' but it's harder to 'let go' and forgive."

"Yes ma'am," I replied. "Momma, can I ask you a

question?"

"Yes."

"Why did everyone clap when Doughboy killed that guy?"

After a slight pause, my mom answers, "Sometimes, the hate we have for each other, as a people, is so strong that you begin to hurt people who look just like you."

"Why momma?"

"When you harm someone who resembles you, internally, there's something about yourself that you don't like."

"Yes ma'am," I replied, acknowledging what my mom was teaching me.

"Plus, Nicholas, when our black boys kill each other, it does two things."

"What's that?"

"For one, it shortens 'our' boy's life expectancy. And, on another note, killing each other only leads our black boys to two places; to jail or in a grave. Those are two places I never want to see you in baby."

"Well momma, I'm going to die one day, right?"

"Yes, eventually you will," replies momma. "But you

never want to put yourself in a position to assist you in dying quicker than expected. A mother's worst fear is burying her child."

"Yes ma'am…I get it…really, I get it."

We pull into our apartment complex and retire for the night. After 'Boyz N the Hood,' my mom would continue to take me to see "our" black movies such as X, Juice, Crooklyn, New Jack City, and Set it Off, to name a few. She wanted to give me a better perspective of why things were as they existed in our neighborhoods.

Growing up, I always enjoyed watching and analyzing these movies with my mom. As I got older, I respected and appreciated my mother much more for doing that. Instead of watching the typical kid movies such as The Lion King or Toy Story, my mom wanted to make sure I was aware of the struggles our people faced in the past, as well as the strife we were to face in the future. Raising a young black man wasn't easy for her, but she understood what it took, and did the absolute best she could.

BATTLE'S BLUEPRINT

The key to being successful is not simply understanding your brilliance. It's understanding how to use your brilliance to affect others.

One Love
Artist: Nas
Album: Illmatic

It was the beginning of my third-grade year at Southern Hills. Mrs. Baptiste was my teacher. I really enjoyed her class because she "looked" just like me. Not that we favored each other, but rather she was black. It was a reassuring figure every day in class. I knew that she understood me, and through her actions, I understood her.

Mrs. Baptiste was the first teacher that truly challenged me because she knew that, as a black man, I needed to work harder than my white counterparts in order to stay "level" and "afloat" with them. Remaining on "equal" ground wasn't in her vision for me. She wanted me to ascend to a higher stratosphere than I could even imagine or comprehend at that moment in my life. She was the first "true" extension of my mother in the classroom.

Although my third-grade year ended successful, with me receiving straight A's for the second year in a row, the first semester was as rocky as any I had. I was eight years old. My mother and I had just lost nearly everything she worked so hard for. Forget thinking about buying school clothes, we were trying to figure out a way to get a couch to sit on. During that moment, I didn't think anything of it. It "was what it was." It was life. Matter of fact, it was our life. We had to handle it or let it handle us. It might have come close to overcoming us, but we're the Battle family. We always went out swinging.

As if everything we were going through wasn't enough, I had to deal with the fact that my dad wasn't there like he should have been. As stated earlier, my dad's Navy stationing was nowhere near me. His first duty station was in Oregon, followed by the Philippians, and then off to Hawaii. As a kid, when hearing that my dad was in Hawaii, I dreamed of him calling me and telling me that he's flying home to Shreveport, just to pick me up, so that I could fly back with him to Hawaii for a couple weeks in the summer. What the hell was I thinking? That shit never happened.

My dad did call me from time-to-time, though. I

remember getting a call every month or two, depending on where I was located at the time. If I was staying with his parents on that weekend, my grandmother would light up like a Christmas tree when she had the opportunity to link the two of us. I guess it was her way of feeling as if my dad was fulfilling his "fatherly" duties.

When the school year began, either my mom or my PawPaw and grandmother would buy school clothes for me. If my grandmother did, she would always tell me, "These are from your dad!" As a gullible child, I would smile with enjoyment, thinking these came from him. I could see the look of disgust on my mom's face when I would reiterate what my grandmother told me. I would originally think it was because of jealousy, but as I got older, I realized it was because she knew who really bought them. She would just smile and nod her head, though, resisting any confrontation.

When I needed sports equipment to participate in all the activities my mom had me involved in, I never received any of it from him. Hell, he never came to just one of my sporting events…ever. My mom did that. When I sit back and analyze the benefits of me attending an out-of-zone elementary school, the quality of education was a huge selling factor;

however, the downside to the whole ordeal was many of the kids I went to school with did not have the same family structure as I   did. My mom was more than likely the only single-parent at all my sporting events. She was 'mom' and 'dad' all the time.

Even through all the financial hardships and misdealt hands my mom endured in life, she never once requested child support from my father. She would always say that she was not going to make a grown ass man take care of his child. If my dad truly wanted to assure my wellbeing on his accord, he could have easily sent a check every month to my mom. It could have been as little as $50. At a minimum, I would have known that he, at least, attempted to provide for me. Looking back now, all that was on my mother. She didn't have to attempt to do anything…she HAD to do it, no matter what. Oh well. Everything happens for a reason.

I had two best friends at Southern Hills…Stuart and Trey. Both came from a two-parent household. Stuart's family was cool as hell. He lived not too far from the school. We'd have sleepovers at his house on different occasions and have a blast. From eating the local Johnny's Pizza chain, to playing video games, to shooting hoops, or just running around like crazy little kids in his backyard, we made the best out of all our moments.

Trey's dad was my elementary football coach. We used to have practice at the nearby football fields or at Trey's house. His backyard was large with a trampoline. I would always lie to my mom concerning what time practice would start, usually saying it began 30 minutes earlier than it did just so I could hop on the trampoline with Trey. When we had sleepovers at his house, we'd do the same as if we were at Stuart's; however, instead of ordering Johnny's pizza, Trey's mom made these homemade pizzas that I still remember to this day. Trey's mom, Mrs. Deb was a true gem!

I enjoyed hanging with my boys because I saw their life as perfect. Both families were, in my eyes, structured right. Their parents…not parent…were amazing, and because of that, I always felt like I had to try to make it seem as though my dad's absence in my life was for some amazing reason.

"My dad's in the Navy…fighting wars," I would sometimes say with a fake smile on my face; not knowing that our country wasn't even at war during that time.

Other times, I might say "He's off at sea…catching fish," because, through my logic, if he's in the Navy, he must be on a ship in the ocean. If he's in the ocean, he must be fishing. Get my drift? Man-oh-man, how simple a child's mind thinks. It's kind of humorous and sad at the same time; however, these are the things I felt, as an eight-year-old, I had to do in order to seem as if I were normal.

The same reasons I felt abnormal when it came to Stuart and Trey, in regards to my paternal situation, are the same reasons I was excited at the start of my third-grade school year. My dad was set to get married to my future stepmom, Sarah, at the end of the August. I couldn't wait to tell my boys to validate everything I had said about my father. Yes…he was in the Navy. And yes…he's a real person. Stuart and Trey probably didn't give a damn about whether my dad was who I said he was. We were kids. All they probably cared about was whether we'd be playing NBA Jam later during the day. Although, it may not have mattered to them, it did matter to have some sort of "inclusion" into a semi two-parent home.

My dad and Sarah's relationship seemed to be destined for a union together. Both were in the Navy, stationed in Hawaii together. However, the coincidence of their relationship was that both were natives from Shreveport.

Sarah was from a neighborhood on the Northside of town called the Cooper Road, and of course, my dad was from Motown. Both had recently got out of the military and settled in Dallas together for a couple years prior to their marriage.

My dad and Sarah's wedding was on August 31, 1991. I was the ring bearer, dressed in a miniature white tuxedo matching my dad's. It was a beautiful ceremony. My grandparents were there on the front row and Sarah's parents, Mr. and Mrs. Richardson, sat on the opposite pew. The wedding was just like any other…vows, kiss, and then exit to the reception where the fun would begin. Sarah's siblings, Junior and Phyliss, were the life of the party, especially Junior. They were like another uncle and aunt to me. The Richardson family was now my new "other" family and they were exactly what I needed at that time. With Sarah now in the fold, I felt my dad's return to Shreveport happening more often throughout the year. I figured this would ultimately be the time in which my dad could finally watch me grow.

Real Friends
Artist: Kanye West (Feat TY$)
Album: The Life of Pablo

As my dad and Sarah were settling down within their newly formed marriage, my mother remained single most of my childhood. Most children of single parents may not be able to say this, but I can honestly say that I had never seen my mom date anyone. She didn't have boyfriends living at our apartment. She never believed in the concept of "shacking up" with your partner. I'm sure she went out on dates with guys; however, she kept that portion of her life separate from me. I get "it." No child, especially a son, wants to have an unpleasant view of who their mother was or what she represented. My mom did a great job of shielding whatever lifestyle she had, outside of being a parent, from me. Shit, for all I know, my mom was the Virgin Mary...even if I know it's not true. But I'd rather have that image of her than the opposite.

A couple years had now passed, and I was now in the fifth grade. It was my last year at Southern Hills. Fifth grade brought me to Mrs. Pat Beauchamp's class. Without a doubt,

Mrs. Beauchamp was my all-time favorite teacher. I know, in my heart, that she truly loved and cared for me.

Mrs. Beauchamp saw that my mom was a single parent. She understood the steps that my mom had to take to assure I was prepared for class. My mom never missed a parent-teacher meeting. She assured that I never missed a day of class. I had flawless grades, perfect attendance, and always paid close attention to what Mrs. Beauchamp presented to us. I appreciated her, and I know she appreciated me for my actions throughout the school year.

Towards the end of the school year, we had an after-school science fair to showcase some things we had created in class. As usual, my mom came...by herself. It never really bothered me until this day for some reason. I had been at Southern Hills four years now, and my situation at home had yet to change. Many of my classmates had both parents at this event. I just always wondered why I didn't. I left the event that night with a whirlwind of thoughts in my head.

"Is this how life is always going to be," I thought to myself. "Will it always be just me and mom," I contemplated.

"Why was my dad blessed to have a significant other, but

my mom wasn't," I thought.

"Is it normal for an eleven-year-old child to be the man of the house," I wondered.

My fifth-grade year was near completion. My thoughts should have focused on my successful journey through Southern Hills. Video games and sports should've occupied my time. My focus should have shifted to what middle school I would be attending. Instead, the thoughts I experienced during that car ride home the previous night pestered me. My mother was a beautiful woman and had sacrificed so much for me. I had a stepmom in Sarah, but when and where would I find my stepdad?

"Mom," I said. "When are you going to get a boyfriend? Everybody else's mother has, at least a boyfriend…"

"Boy, hush…"

"For real momma…Don't you want someone to help out around here?"

"Look," she replied. "I don't need anyone to 'help' me with anything, whether it's you, or the bills, or whatever."

With a confused look on my face, I ask, "But, why?"

"Nicholas," she said as she turned towards me. "Don't you ever depend on anyone for anything. If you can't get it by yourself, then you don't need it. If you want something, then work hard for it and get it…Ok?"

BATTLE'S BLUEPRINT
Never acquire things you do not need to impress people you do not like.

"Yes ma'am," I replied. I thought about what she said for a quick second. For as little as we had, I never recalled my mother feeling sorry for ourselves. She was proud…sometimes too proud. I often thought if it lessened our opportunity to receive what one might possibly perceive as a "blessing." I couldn't worry about that, though. I trusted my momma, and if she abided by these principles, then it must have been correct.

The school year was now over. While my mom was away at work, I would either stay home during the day or go to one of my grandparent's houses. If I stayed home, my instructions were to keep the house clean, never answer the door unless I was expecting a family member to come, and never answer the phone unless it was someone I knew. If family were in the process of leaving a message on our answering machine, then answering was OK. One morning, our phone rang…*Ring, Ring!*

The answering machine clicks on and an uncommon voice begins to speak. "Billie, uhhh…this is Larry…uhhh…from a few years ago."

There was a brief pause before the man begins to speak again.

"Well, I just wanted to try to reconnect with you and…uhhh…let you know that I live in Texas now. Call me back if you want…my number is 254-618…"

The man hung up the phone on his end and I looked at the answering machine as if I had just saw a ghost appear from it. Who in the hell is *'Larry'* from a *'few years ago?'*

As if I was the adult in the household, I started hyping myself up, pacing through the house and spewing questions in the air.

"Wait till she gets home," I said. "Who is Larry? First off, what kind of name is Larry?"

"And he said he knew her from a *'few years back'*," I said. "How you gonna meet a guy a few years back and I don't know who he is?"

I walked through the house mad. I felt betrayed. We had

a system in our apartment. I was the man of the house, or so I thought. Now, some dude named 'Larry' was about to threaten my throne.

I glance at the clock. It's now 2:30pm. My mom gets off work in an hour. I go to my room to play a video game, but I just wasn't feeling it. I was ready to talk to my mom about 'Larry.' Thirty minutes passes by and the front door of the apartment begins to open.

"Heyyyyyy," my mom yells as she passes through the living room.

"Momma…uhh…you're home early," I replied in a startled and surprised voice.

"Yea…I got off early today. Did you take those beef tips out the freezer like I asked?"

"Yes ma'am. It's in the sink."

"Good," she replies as she walks back to her room to change clothes. "Anybody call?" she asks.

For all the tough talking I thought I was going to do, I just simply replied, "Uhhhh…. yes ma'am."

"Who was it?"

I didn't answer. I went completely silent.

"Nicholas," my mom restated. "Did you hear me? Who

called?"

"Uhh…I don't know."

My mom goes over to the answering machine by her bed and presses the button to retrieve her messages. She hears the message from 'Larry' in its entirety. I was ease dropping from my room, which was directly across from my mom's room, before hearing her break her silence.

"A few years," she mocked. "Try five or six years."

My mom begins to walk towards her bedroom door in order to get to the kitchen. As I hear her feet march across the floor, I quickly, yet quietly, move from the edge of my door to my bed behind me…impersonating playing a video game. My mom didn't mention anything about this mysterious 'Larry' as she goes to the kitchen.

As if the phone call never happened, my mother yells out, "Nicholas…rice or mashed potatoes?"

"Rice," I say as I start to walk towards the kitchen. I get to the kitchen door and stand there as my mom starts to brown the beef tips.

"Momma," I said. "Who is Larry?"

"No one," she sharply replies. "Just an old

friend."

"Boyfriend," I ask in an awkwardly shallow voice.

"Boy, mind your business. And no, he's not my boyfriend."

"Ok, but momma," I said. "He said he knew you from a…"

"Hush!"

"Yes ma'am," I said as I sat at our table anticipating dinner. My angry inner 'Machoman Randy Savage' fighting spirit was down to an attitude like a miniature chihuahua. Sure, I might have yapped and thought I was accomplishing something; however, when you realize momma was a full-grown Doberman Pincher, you immediately understand you ain't shit!

I ate my dinner that night, and hardly ever thought about the mysterious call from 'Larry.' A couple weeks had passed. My mom and I were watching TV on a Friday night. It was our normal Friday evening. We ordered pizza from Johnny's and watched the T.G.I.F. series of shows on ABC. Family Matters, Full House, and Step-by-Step were our normal rotation of shows to watch. Halfway through 'Family

Matters,' the phone rings. As with any kid in my era, I ran to go answer the phone.

"I got it…I got it," I said, as I ran over to the phone. I answer the phone, "Hello?"

"Hello, is Billie there," said a semi-familiar voice.

I would usually just hand the phone over to my mom, but this person called my mom 'Billie,' and nobody calls my mom 'Billie.' It's 'Renee.' Plus, the voice sounded too familiar, but I couldn't put my finger on who the person on the other end of the phone was. So instead of handing the phone over to my mom, I got nosey as hell.

"May I ask who's calling," I said.

"Larry."

"Just a minute," I replied…but I thought, "Aww Hell Naw!"

"Nicholas, who is it," said my mom.

I walk over and hand her the phone. "It's Larry."

My mom takes the cordless phone, and says hello as she walks into her room. I wanted to know what she was going to say to the mystery guy without looking too suspicious. Since my mom's bedroom shared a wall with our apartment's bathroom, I 'suddenly' had to go use the bathroom. I go into the bathroom and sit on the toilet. As I sat, I quietly leaned forward to see if I could hear anything from their conversation.

"Wow…" says mom in as sarcastic of a voice as possible. "Never thought I'd hear from you again!"

She continues to spout out muffled rhetoric to this 'Larry' fella that I couldn't understand. I begin to get up until I could clearly hear my mom's voice again.

Semi-angrily, she tells 'Larry,' "I'll go on a date with you next weekend on two conditions. You come down here on Saturday, and you get yourself a hotel room. You are NOT, and I repeat, NOT staying with me!"

More small talk occurs before my mom says bye. As soon as I hear the 'B' in bye, I simultaneously flush the toilet as if I really had done something in the bathroom. I hear my mom open her door and walk back into the living room.

"Nicholas," she yelled.

"Coming…just washing my hands," I replied.

I finish 'fake' washing my hands before coming back into the living room. We continue to watch the T.G.I.F. television shows before heading off to bed. That night, I didn't know what to think. I've never seen or known my mom to have a boyfriend, let alone go out on a date. Oh well, next week couldn't get here fast enough.

The days leading up to my mom's upcoming date passed painfully slow. A lot of questions ran through my head.

"What did Larry look like," I thought.

"Why was he in Texas and not in Shreveport?"

"What part of Texas was he in," I pondered. "Maybe he's in Dallas, and if my mom starts dating him, we could visit him and I'd be in the same city as my dad more often to see him."

It was now Friday and me and mom went through our normal Friday routine of ABC's T.G.I.F. shows and Johnny's Pizza. All week, there was no mention of Larry or their date. As I sit on the floor, in front of the couch, my mom comes to sit down on the couch.

"Nicholas, go get me the phone."

"Yes ma'am," I said as I retrieve the phone and bring it to her.

"Thank you, baby," she says as she dials a phone number. The person on the other end answers and my mom beings to speak.

"Hey, what you doing girl," my mom says.

I heard a loud voice on the other end. That could be only my cousin BC. After a few minutes of talking, it was easy to realize that was exactly who was on the other line.

"Girl, what are you doing tomorrow night," says momma.

After some small talk, I hear my mom saying she'd see BC tomorrow afternoon. She hangs the phone up and begins to talk to me.

"Nicholas, BC's coming over tomorrow to watch you for a while," she says.

"Is she spending the night?"

"Maybe," my mom replies. "But I'll be home after a couple hours. I'm just going out to dinner."

"Ok," I said, as I contain myself from asking any further questions.

We finish up T.G.I.F. and the rest of the large pepperoni pizza before heading off to bed. As we start to go sleep, we hear a knock at the door. My head jumps off my pillow and my mom walked to the front door in a bit of a frenzy.

She peeks out of our living room window and sees BC's red Hyundai Excel. She opens the door and begins fussing like a typical "momma-bear" would.

"Girl, it's ten o'clock!"

"I know," BC says as she walks in the house. "I was already on this side of town and instead of me driving all the way back to Moorningsport tonight, just to come right back here tomorrow, I just said I'd come over now."

My mom looks at BC with the side-eye before going to the linen closet and handing her a blanket.

"Get Nicholas up," BC tells my mom.

"Girl, that boy is sleep."

"But I brought some Southern Maid," she said.

That's all I had to hear. I got out the bed on my own and walked in the living room.

"Boy, what are you doing up," says my mom.

"Well…I heard Southern Maid!"

My mom looked and shook her head before letting out a halfway laugh. BC followed, but her laugh was never halfway. It was full throttle. Mom turned the TV back on and we watched a taped re-run of "In Living Color" while we ate the donuts BC brought over. Before I knew it, I was out cold and Saturday was upon us.

Since we had a late night, we all woke up a little later than usual. We all ate a little breakfast before BC and I left to go to the mall. She did some shoe-shopping before we stopped by the arcade so that Ronny could give me some free games. After leaving the arcade, we head to Southern Classic Chicken, followed by Southern Maid Donuts…again. We get back home in the late afternoon, right before my mom applied the finishing touches to her makeup. A few minutes later, she grabs her purse and heads out for her dinner.

BC and I just chilled at the apartment that night. We rented a few movies from Blockbuster and watched them until my mom came home, just shy of 9pm.

"Hey black people," my mom says as she walks through the door.

"Hey momma."

"Hey Renee," says BC.

"What did y'all eat," my mom asks as she walks towards the kitchen.

"Some Classic and Southern Maid," replies BC. "I bought an eight piece with some mashed potatoes. It's some still in there."

"I'm good," says my mom before going to her room to change clothes.

We all watched a little bit of TV before going to bed. This would become our normal routine, it seemed like, every other week. BC would keep me Saturday afternoon while mom went out to dinner. Mom comes back home after a few hours and we all watch movies or TV.

My mom comes home after work on a Friday night. As we eat our normal Friday night dinner of Johnny's pizza, she begins to asks me a few questions.

"Baby, how would you feel if momma had a boyfriend," she asks.

"I don't know," I replied.

"Do you not know because you don't want mom to have a boyfriend, or do you not know because you've never seen mom with a boyfriend?"

"Both," I said with a slight grin.

"Well, I have someone I want you to meet tomorrow."

"Who," I said with a raised eyebrow, already knowing the answer.

"My friend Larry."

"Oh…ok," I replied as if I were in shock. I already mentally got over the fact that my mom was dating someone, so I was now more worried about not getting free arcade tokens from Ronny at the arcade every other week.

"He's going to come pick us up tomorrow and take us

out to dinner."

"Ok," I replied.

"Alright, momma needs to know how you like him…or not," she says. "Ok?"

"Ok, momma," I say as I continue to eat my strip of pizza before heading off to bed. Tomorrow couldn't get here any sooner now!

It's now Saturday around three o'clock in the afternoon. My mom's getting ready.

"Nicholas," she yells from her room. "Go iron your clothes and get ready. I told Larry we'd be ready around four."

"Ok," I said, as I pick out my favorite outfit my mom bought me. It was a pair of dark money green 'Guess' Jeans with a striped cream and green 'Guess' shirt. Since the Dallas Cowboys were my favorite team, my mom bought me a pair of Emmitt Smith Reeboks shoes the prior Christmas. I ironed my outfit, put my clothes on, and I was ready. My mom puts on some jeans and a nice shirt; nothing too fancy. We were just going to get something to eat. It's now 3:50PM and my mom and I go to the living room and wait. A few minutes later, someone knocks on our door.

'Knock…Knock…Knock.'

"Just a minute," my mom says. She opens the door and I peek around her to get a glimpse of 'Larry.' As I get to see the man behind the door, my eyes got big and I was semi-speechless. Larry was a white dude. I mean full-fledged white…not Louisiana creole white…I mean "Danny Tanner" from "Full House" white.

Larry was a bigger guy…not big as in fat, but big as in muscular. He was about 6 foot 2 inches and around 230 pounds. He was a physically imposing guy…no doubt.

"You must be Nicholas," he says in a deep voice. Still in amazement by the obvious, I reply,

"Yes."

"Nice to meet you," he says as he shakes my hand.

"Ok," says my mom, as she can see I'm still a little in shock. "Let's go eat."

We walk outside and I saw one car in the parking lot that I did not recognize. It was a blue 1987 Chevy Monte Carlo SS. Now, I didn't know much about Larry, but if this was his car, he was already starting off on the right foot. You see, in Louisiana, if you had an Oldsmobile Cutlass, Chevy Monte Carlo, or a Buick Regal, you were "the man," especially in the neighborhoods I grew up in.

Hoping that this Monte Carlo was Larry's, he walks over to the passenger side of the car, opens the door, and pulls the seat back before telling me to get in. I load into the back seat and he puts the front seat back in its normal position before my mom gets in the front seat. Larry closes the door, hops in the driver's seat and we head off to get dinner.

We arrive at a local diner and sit down for dinner. Although it was in the early 1990's, interracial dating was not a common thing in Shreveport. The city, for the most part, was "black" and "white" with no grey area in between. As we sit, I can notice the eyes staring at us. It was an uncomfortable feeling for me, so I could only imagine how Larry must have felt, coming into unchartered territory in the 'Deep South' to date a black woman. If it bothered him, he didn't let it show. He was as comfortable around 'my' people, just as I was. That was his first 'check' on my mental progress report I had for him.

"So, Nicholas," Larry says. "You're in fifth grade, right?"

"Yep," I replied before my mom gave me a sharp look out the corner of here eye.

"I mean, yes sir," I quickly corrected myself. "I just finished fifth grade and am going into sixth grade this year."

"What middle school will you be going to?"

"Well," I thought. "I'm supposed to go to Turner Middle School, but my mom wants me to take an entry exam to try to go to Caddo Middle Magnet."

"Yes," my mom interrupts. "That's right. You'll get in baby."

"I hope so," I replied.

"I'm sure you'll get it buddy," Larry said before taking a sip of water.

"Mr. Larry," I stated. "What do you do?"

Looking a little confused, he repeats my question. "What do I do?"

"Yes sir…like, what is your job?"

"Well, I'm in the Army."

"Ok…is your Army base here in Shreveport?"

"No," Larry replies. "I live in Texas…Fort Hood, Texas."

"How far is that from here," I ask.

"About a five-hour drive," replies Larry.

"Five hourrsssss...that sure is a long drive," I reply as our waitress comes to the table to refill our glasses with water.

"Well," Larry says, "Your mom is special, and special people deserve effort."

"Welllll," I replied. "Since I'm the man of the house, do you have to put in some effort with me too?"

With a chuckle, Larry proceeds, "Yes…yes I do. So, what should we do?"

"Swimming," I replied with an excited tone in my voice and an enthusiastic look on my face.

"So, swimming it is!"

"Yessssss…. swimming it is!"

I glance at my mom and see that she's enjoying the conversation Larry and I are having. Hell, she was probably more nervous about this encounter than either of us because if our meeting did not go well, this may have been the last time any of us would have seen Larry.

We continue with dinner before Larry drives us back home. My mom and I get out of the car and Larry walk us to the front door. He gives me a "high-five" and my mom a hug before getting into his car and leaving to go to his hotel.

"Nicholas," says my mom. "So how did you like Larry?"

"He's cool momma. I think he's pretty cool."

"Well, good. I'm glad you two hit it off well."

"You just make sure he's ready to go swimming the next time he comes down," I sarcastically say.

My mom laughingly replies, "Will do!" The look on my mom's face revealed of huge sigh of relief. Being that this was the first guy she had ever felt comfortable enough to introduce me to, my mom was just glad this day was a success and finally over with.

Summertime (In the LBC)
Artist: The Dove Shack
Album: This is the Shack

It was Friday morning, and just two weeks earlier, Larry told me that he would take me swimming the next time he came to Shreveport. He called the house earlier, around 5AM, before he left his house in Killeen, Texas, so he'd be at our apartment around 10AM. My mom was getting ready for work, and had to leave soon. Today was going to be the first time Larry and I would have some "alone" time. I'm scrambling through my dresser drawers looking for my swimming trunks with no success.

"Momma," I yelled. "Have you seen my swimming trunks?"

"Check your closet. They should be folded on the top shelf."

"Ok," I replied. "They ain't there momma!"

"Did you check in your bottom dresser?"

"Yes ma'am…"

"Check again…"

I checked the bottom drawer and didn't see my trunks. As I close the drawer, I noticed the drawer didn't close all the way. It felt like a cushion was behind it. I pull out my bottom drawer to see what was behind it. There were my trunks!

"Found 'em," I shouted to mom.

"Good…now I'm off to work," replied my mom. "Larry will be here in a few hours. Don't you open the door for no one else but him."

"Ok."

My mom opens the door to start walking to her car.

"Behave yourself," she says. "I love you."

"Love you too momma."

I close and lock the door before going to my room to play a few video games. I begin to play my "Streets of Rage" video game on my Sega Genesis. I play for a couple hours, neglecting eating breakfast, before I hear a knock on the door. It was only 9:30AM, so Larry wasn't supposed to be here yet. I peak out of the living room window and see Larry's Monte Carlo. I go and open the door.

"What's up buddy," said Larry.

"Hey man!"

Larry comes into the house. I pick up the phone and call mom.

"Human Resources department. This is Billie. How may I direct your call?"

"Hey momma, it's me."

"Hey baby, what's up?"

"Larry made it in."

"Oh...," she replied. "That was quick. Put him on the phone please."

I hand the phone over to Larry. He and my mom talk for

a few minutes before he hands the phone back to me.

"Hello," I say.

"Hey baby…have fun and call me if you need anything. Love you."

"Love you too," I reply as I hang up the phone.

It was now just Larry and I in the house. To break the silence, Larry began small talk with me.

"Are you hungry buddy?"

"I can eat," I say enthusiastically.

"What do you want to eat?"

"McDonald's is across the street," I reply. "Wanna go there?"

"Sure."

We hop in Larry's car and drive across the street to McDonalds. As we enter the restaurant, I knew exactly what I wanted. We head to the counter.

"Welcome to McDonalds. How may I help you?", said the girl at the cash register.

"Ummmm…Can I have a hotcakes and sausage…and a large orange juice please?"

"Anything else?"

"And a hash brown, please."

"Sir," the girl says to Larry. "And for you?"

"I'll take a number one with a coffee."

"Ok...So I have a hotcakes and sausage with a hash brown and a large orange juice. A number one with a coffee. Anything else?"

"That's it," replies Larry as the girl hands us our food and drinks before we go to sit down inside the restaurant.

As we begin to eat, me and Larry start talking about sports. "So, your mom says you're a Cowboys fan."

"Yep," I replied.

"How'd you become a Cowboys fan with your mom being a Saints fan?"

"My grandma...She loves the Cowboys...and I do too," as I munch on my hotcakes.

"Who's your favorite player?"

"Emmitt Smith...and Irvin. I can't decide between those two. Who's your favorite team," I ask of Larry.

"The Steelers."

"Oh really," I replied. "We play y'all this year. Should be a goooodddd game. Plus, you guys have Bettis and Rod

Woodson. Woodson versus Irvin should be epic!"

Larry begins to chuckle a little. "You really like sports, huh?"

"Like? I love it," I reply laughing.

Larry and I continue to talk about sports as we eat our breakfast. We talked about basketball and even more football. Although I'm not a big baseball fan, we even talked about that also. Larry grew up in the Cleveland area and was a huge Indians fan. Cleveland's up-and-coming star, Albert Joey Belle, was from Shreveport, and Larry had no idea.

"Can't believe an eleven-year-old is teaching me about baseball," laughs Larry.

"What can I say…what can I say…," I jokingly tell Larry.

We finish up and head back to get ready to go to the pool at the apartments. It was high noon and Larry had to worry about something I was not privy to…sunburn.

"Nicholas," Larry says. "Do you want to wait a little bit before we go swimming?"

"Nope…I'm ready man!"

Uneasily looking at the Louisiana heat bouncing off the pavement outside, Larry grabs a couple of towels and heads out the door.

"Well, let's go then," he replied with a smile on his face.

I run to the pool and Larry hurriedly walks behind me. We get to the pool and I cannon ball in! Larry jumps in also. We swim for an hour or so before Larry gets out and lays out on one of the beach chairs.

The sun was scorching hot that day so I continued to stay in the pool. I grabbed my snorkel to keep swimming. The temperature got a little hotter and the back of my neck began to feel the heat. I get out the pool and see that Larry had now turned over to lay on his stomach in the beach chair.

"Larry, you ready to go?"

"Only if you are buddy."

"Yea, let's go…"

Larry and I got out the pool and went back to the apartment. I showered and grabbed some lunch from the refrigerator. Larry showered and laid on the couch to get some rest. The sun must have exhausted him because he went to sleep almost immediately. I w e n t back in my room and finished my "Streets of Rage" video game before my mom made it home.

"Hey," my mom says as she walks in the house and notices Larry sleep on the couch.

"What's up," replies a hazy Larry.

I ran into the living room. "Hey momma!"

"Hey baby, how was swimming?"

"Fun, fun, fun," I replied.

"Sunburned, sunburned, sunburned," replied a laughing Larry.

"Ohhhh," my mom says with a wincing face.

"Sunburn," I reply. "You got sunburn?"

"Aww, don't worry about it buddy," said Larry.

I felt kind of bad that Larry got sunburned while swimming with me; however, in a crazy way, Larry's sunburned skin sort of symbolized his selflessness and willingness to put me first. Maybe he was just crazy for not putting on sunscreen before we left the apartment, but all he wanted me to do was have fun…and that's what we did.

From that moment on, Larry was A-Okay with me. He was my dude. I liked and trusted him; and I knew that he had my back…and I had his also. More importantly, I trusted him with my mom. She deserved a good guy, and if that meant I might have to relinquish some of the "man of the house" duties in the near-future, then I was cool with that. Until then though, Larry had a few more McDonald's breakfasts and pool trip weekends to truly solidify himself,

but he was well on the right path, at least in my eyes.

TRACK #5: YOU'RE ALL I NEED

Artist: Method Man

Album: Tical

One of the most soulful songs I have ever heard.

Of course, Method Man was speaking of a woman as he composed this song. However, as a youth, Hip-Hop was my girl. She was all I needed to "get by." She was my "sweet morning dew." She was my "destiny."

Hip-Hop helped me get through certain periods of my life. She also brought new additions to my life, and for that, I love you Hip-Hop.

As a youth, there were a few moments throughout the year that I looked forward to. My first big event on my calendar was Thanksgiving because, with both sides of my family residing in Shreveport, I had plenty of houses to go and eat at. My grandmother Mattie made a strawberry cake to die for and her sister, my aunt Louis, made pound cakes, pies, pickled peaches, and just about anything else that tasted good. My grandmother Vergie made the best dressing and pecan pies you could ever want.

Christmas was my next favorite event to wait for. Every year, my cousin Jay and I would meet up at PawPaw's house and bring all our new video games we got. When Sega Genesis was the featured game console, we got every upgrade for it. Sega CD was our new toy one year. I got "Sonic CD" and Jay got "Joe Montana's Football." We'd stay up all night and into the early morning playing video games; only taking small rest breaks to drink the Country Time Lemonade and Nestea PawPaw would buy us every weekend.

As enjoyable as these two days were, the moment I waited for the most was the week or two I would visit my dad when my school year finished, especially the summer of

1994 when my dad and Sarah bought their house in Dallas. I remember when the house was under construction. The first time I saw the finished product, I was ecstatic because the environment that my dad and Sarah could potentially provide me rivaled, and possibly bested, some of the living situations of the kids I went to school with. I immediately imagined myself in the house. I had my room picked out and everything. It just felt like "home."

I just finished my fifth-grade year at Southern Hills. I rushed out of my class to go to the front and wait for my PawPaw to pick me up from school. I look around; however, there was no PawPaw anywhere. I then see my PawPaw's van pull up to the loading zone curb, but as I veered through the window, the person driving the car didn't look like PawPaw. As the van approaches and stops, the window rolls down and a familiar voice speaks to me.

"What's up playa," says the voice.

As I glare into the van, I realized exactly who owned that voice.

"Uncle Rod," I replied in sheer enjoyment. I opened the van's door and hopped in. Uncle Rod and my Aunt Vickie were both in the Air Force, stationed in Japan at the time, so whenever he was able to come into town, I made sure I went to PawPaw's house.

"What's up Unc," I said. "I thought you and Auntie Vickie weren't coming for another couple of days?"

"Momma got the date wrong," he replied. "Her and Earl were just as shocked to see us come through the door this morning too!"

"How long are y'all staying?"

"A couple weeks."

"Cool," I replied as we started our way back home. "PawPaw's taking me to my Dad's house tomorrow."

"I know. He told me. I'm going to ride down there tomorrow with y'all."

"Ok.".

We pulled into my grandmother and PawPaw's house. Since I already knew I was going to my Dad's the next day, my mom packed my bag and brought it to the house the day before. I was completely ready to make my way down to my dad's house the next morning. I couldn't wait.

As the morning sunrise sprung, my PawPaw woke me up because he wanted to get on the road early.

"Nicholas! Wake up and brush your teeth so we can go."

"Ok…Ok PawPaw," I replied as I got out the bed. I stand in front of the bathroom sink as I wash my face and brush my teeth. I go to my room and put my clothes on before grabbing my suitcase to put in PawPaw's van. As I get to the van, I noticed my Uncle Rod was already inside it. He loved to drive, so a three-hour trip to Dallas was a no-brainer "ride" for him. Grandma, PawPaw, Aunt Vickie, and myself all loaded into the van and began our trip to my dad's house.

After an early morning wakeup, I instantly dozed back off to sleep as the van reached I-20 towards Dallas. When I woke up, it felt like I had been asleep for a short time; however, we were exiting off the Wheatland Road exit in Dallas, just minutes from my dad's house. We pull into the driveway and my dad's burgundy Honda Accord was outside. His garage door was open, with him sitting in a foldable chair inside it. We park and get out the car.

"What up Dad!"

"What's up man," he replied. "Go put your suitcase in the bedroom."

"Ok," I said as I walked into the house. I pass the kitchen and enter straight into the living room where my stepmother, Sarah, was sitting on their white leather couch with my newborn baby sister, Carlena.

"Hey Sarah," I whispered, as my sister was sleep in her arms.

"Hey Nicholas," she replied as I reached down and gave her hug before I headed off to my bedroom to put my suitcase in the closet.

One thing I loved about my bedroom at my dad's house was the king-sized bed it had in it with a mirror in the headboard and multiple compartments that I could hide my toys in. In front of the bed was a dresser with a thirty-inch tube television on top of it. It was far different than the full-size bed and small wooden nightstand I was accustomed to in my mom's apartment. After seeing the differences in living situations, I could picture myself at my dad's house full-time. I could get used to this.

My grandparents, aunt, and uncle left my dad's house that afternoon on their way back to Shreveport. I sat on the couch next to my dad and Sarah. My sister lay snuggly in a blanket next to me. As I sat there on the couch, I began to wonder if this is where I needed to be.

Simple Things
Artist: Nas
Album: NASIR

During my week at my dad's house, he and Sarah would go to work during the day while I stayed at the house. I never minded it though because my dad had a huge satellite in his backyard that allowed us to pick up nearly every channel imaginable.

With me being a "hip-hop" baby and all, I enjoyed watching "The Box" music video channel that showcased every rap and hip-hop video out. There was 2 Pac, Nas, Outkast, Warren G, MC Eiht, Da Brat, The Fugees, UGK, and countless other videos. I was already in love with music, but the opportunity to put faces to the music I constantly heard made me more of a fan than I already was.

Although the videos were just on constant rotation, I would just sit on the green-carpeted floors and watch every video on repeat. Whether it was Warren G and Nate Dogg's "Regulator" or Nas' "One Love" video, I began to connect with music at a rate higher than any other vice I could imagine. This is where I began to fall in love with Hip-Hop.

With the videos playing the background, I would do the same things at my dad's house my mom taught me. Since my mom worked hard to provide for me, she gave me chores to accomplish while I was at home. Mom was responsible for making sure I was taken great care of. I was responsible for keeping the kitchen, living room, bathroom, and my bedroom clean. In all honesty, it was a fair trade-off.

Da Brat's "Funkdafied" video was playing in the background as I began washing the dishes in the sink from the night before.

"Soooo…. Soooo…Soooo…Funkdafied," I sang as I rinsed the pan Sarah had used the night before to cook her famous Mexican casserole.

I transitioned to the living room to vacuum the floor as Craig Mack's "Flava in Ya Ear" video came on. Some kids might call it work; however, I looked at it as my job. My mom told me to make my dad and Sarah's life easier while I was visiting. That was my mission and I hoped to accomplish that.

While I was singing and cleaning, my dad and Sarah were having a different conversation. Sarah called my dad at his job to talk for a bit.

"This is Carlos," my dad said as his work phone rang.

"Carlos…this is Sarah."

"Hey."

"Hey…uhhh…why don't you call Nicholas and have him wash those dishes in the kitchen."

"Huh? Uhhh…ok," replied my dad, seemingly to please his wife. "I'll call him."

"Ok…that's all I wanted."

"Ok."

My dad hung up the phone and began to dial the house phone to talk to me. *Ring…Ring.*

"Hello."

"Slick Nick!"

"Hey Dad," I replied.

"Hey…why don't you do your old man a favor and knock those dishes out in the kitchen for me."

"Already did them Dad!"

"Oh really," said my dad in an amazed voice. "Well cool. That's all I wanted. I'll be home early tonight. What do you want to eat?"

"Can we have that Braum's burger place again?"

"Cool…we can do that."

"Aight dad…see you when you get home."

We hung up the phone and I continued to watch music videos until Sarah and my dad came home. We went out to dinner that night for burgers before coming back home to get some sleep for the night.

As the morning came, I continued with my normal routine of keeping my portion of the house clean. Life was good. At home in Shreveport, I didn't even have cable, but here, I had over a hundred channels on a satellite. The week was about to end, and I'll admit, I was a little sad to leave. I had a great time and wanted to stay longer if I could, but PawPaw and grandma were on their way in the morning to come and get me.

As they say, all good things must come to an end. My grandparents pulled into my dad's driveway in PawPaw's white van. They came inside the house to relax for a little bit before we loaded back into the van and made our way back to Shreveport. As usual, as soon as the tires hit the pavement, I was out like a light until we made it to our exit in Shreveport, just a short four miles from my grandparent's house.

As we arrive at the house and walked through the door, I see Uncle Rod sitting on the couch watching TV.

"What's up Unc!"

"What's up playa!"

"Nothing much. When are y'all leaving to go back to your military base?"

"Damn playa," Uncle Rod replied jokingly. "You trying to get rid of us already?"

"Naw Unc," I said laughing.

"Oh…your mom called and said to call her once you get in."

"Ok," I replied as I walked over to the phone to call my mom.

As the phone rang, I wondered what my mom wanted to talk about. I just talked to her yesterday and she was just waiting to see me once I got home.

"Hello?"

"Hey Mom!"

"Hey," mom replied. "So, I heard you've been acting up in Dallas. Sarah called and let me know."

"But momma?!? What did I do?"

"We'll talk when I get to your grandparents," she replied as she hung up the phone.

I hung up the phone and my PawPaw walked into the kitchen where the phone was located. He could see the look on my face to notice that something was wrong with me.

"Shotgun…what's wrong?"

"My momma said…my momma said I'm in trouble," I replied. "She said that Sarah told her I was acting up in Dallas."

"She said Sarah told her that?" PawPaw reiterated.

"Yes Sir," I replied with a scarce tone in my voice.

"Don't worry Shotgun," PawPaw replied. "I got your back. Ain't nothing going to happen to you."

"Ok."

Waiting for my mom to come to my grandparent's house was probably the most stressful thing I had encountered thus far in my life. I had never heard my mother mad at me in that tone ever. It was as if I had embarrassed her while she was not able to observe me. You see, whenever I was away from home, I was an exact reflection of my mother and tried to adhere to the morals and values she taught me.

Although I knew I didn't do anything wrong, I was

somewhat shocked that, for one, Sarah would say something like this about me, and additionally, my mom would believe that I acted in a disrespectful manner. I did not know how my mother was going to react once she reached the house; however, I had to prepare for whatever she had in store because her champagne colored Honda Accord had just pulled into my grandparent's driveway.

I could feel my heart beat out of my chest as I heard my mom's car door shut close. Her hard-bottomed shoes knocked hard against my grandparent's pavement as she walked up to the front door. My mom opened the door and began immediately fussing at me.

"Nicholas! You know I didn't raise you to act up at other folk's houses!"

"But Momma…" I eagerly replied.

"Get your bag," my momma yelled, "and get your ass in the car. And I mean now!"

"Yes ma'am…"

"And hurry up!"

I remember crying at that moment because I know I was going to get in trouble for something I did not do. My tears streamed down my face as my mom continued to lay an onslaught of fusses at me. Out of nowhere, my PawPaw saw the desperation in my eyes. As my mom continued to fuss, he did something I had never seen him do before. With a raised finger at my mom and with one of the meanest looks I had ever seen my PawPaw have; he returned the fussing towards my mom.

"Billie, now don't you come up in here fussing at Nicholas," he said screaming. "My boy didn't do anything wrong and you know it!"

"Mr. Brown, you gotta get that finger out my face!"

"This is my damn house! And ain't nobody gonna come fussing at my boy in my house!"

I was torn. The two people that I adored the most in my life were at complete odds with each other and I did not know how to handle it. My tears dried up and now I was in complete shock. On one hand, I was my mom's only child. I was her baby and she would die for me…literally. On the other hand, I was essentially my PawPaw's third son and he'd kill somebody for me…no lie. I was scared. Being the mediator of this event, my grandma stepped in diffuse the situation.

"Earl…Billie…calm down," she yelled as she grabbed

my PawPaw. "Billie, I don't believe it. Call Sarah!"

PawPaw walked over to the cordless phone and grabbed it off its base. He calls my dad's house and waits for someone to answer.

"Hello," my dad says as he answers the phone.

"Carlos," PawPaw said in a loud voice. "Did Sarah call Billie and tell her Nicholas was acting up at y'all house?"

"What," my dad replied in a confused manner. "Naw, Earl. Nicholas didn't do anything wrong here."

"I know he didn't, but ask her!"

"Sarah," my dad shouted out to Sarah.

"Yesssss," she replied.

"Come here right quick," he told her as she made her way to the phone. "Did you call Billie and tell her Nicholas was acting up around here?"

"I called her but…uhhh…he didn't wash the dishes that one day…"

"You did what…" my dad replied angrily.

"Carlos," PawPaw interjected. "So, she's lying on my boy?"

"Earl…but…"

"Ain't no but," PawPaw replied. "If my boy ain't allowed there then you don't have to worry about me ever coming back down there!"

"But Earl…it don't gotta be like that," my dad continued.

"I'm done talking!"

"But Earl," replied my dad.

"I'm done!" PawPaw replied as he handed the phone to my grandma and went to the living room to sit down and cool off.

"Carlos," my grandmother said in her comforting voice. "I don't know what was done or said, but you have to fix this."

"I know momma."

"You gotta fix this, Carlos."

"I know momma," my dad replied. "Put Nicholas on the phone."

My grandma handed me the phone. I didn't know what to think or how to react. I was in complete shock at what had just happened. My emotions were all over the place. I took the phone and placed it to my ear.

"Hello," I said with a frail voice.

"Nicholas," my dad said. "Are you okay?"

"Yes...but, I thought Sarah loved me," I replied as I began to immediately cry.

BATTLE'S BLUEPRINT
Respect and understanding lead to mutual respect for one-another. Mutual respect leads to a peaceful coexistence necessary for a successful relationship.

As if my dad could feel the tears through the phone, he began to cry also. It was the first time I had experienced any ounce of emotion from my dad. He sobbed, as if I was a child scorn and abused. I felt bad for him because, at this moment, he was stuck between a rock and a hard place. He had to please his oldest child and parents, while also continue to maintain his new marriage.

With a crackling voice, my dad tells me, "Sarah does love you...Ok?"

"Ok," I replied as I handed the phone to my grandma. I immediately ran to my mom and put my arms around her. I started to cry again, not knowing what emotions to feel.

"You ready to go home baby," my mom said as she wrapped her arms around me.

"Can I stay here tonight momma," I replied with a

sniffling nose.

"Ok…go to the bed and calm down…ok?"

"Yes ma'am. I love you," I replied as I walked to the back of the house and went to my grandma and PawPaw's room. I laid down in their bed and put the blanket over my head and remained crying. I heard footsteps walk towards the room I was in.

"Nicholas," my Uncle Rod said. "You alright man?"

"Yea…"

"Ok…it's gonna be alright man."

I laid silently as I wiped my tears from my eyes. I went into the other bedroom and got into the bed, hoping that if I went to sleep, I would have awakened from a bad dream. The problem that existed was that this was not a dream. The reality hit me hard and it hurt.

I didn't know how to carry on with my dad or Sarah after this occurred. In my eyes, it was always the elephant in the room. In fact, we never discussed what happened that night since it occurred. It was a moment in my life in which I would like to forget; however, I can't erase the past. I did forgive my dad and stepmom for what occurred, but I never forgot what happened. It still sticks with me to this day.

As time went on and tempers calmed down, realization set in that neither Sarah or I were going anywhere. Sarah was my stepmom, and eventually became a great one at that, regardless of the situation that occurred. She was my dad's wife and mother of his only daughter and my only sister. I was my dad's oldest child, and no matter what, I wasn't going anywhere either.

Sarah and I had to learn to exist within a common space, and over the years, we did just that. As I got older, our respect for each other grew immensely. I needed her, and she needed me. Over time, my title would eventually transition from "stepson" to her "oldest son," and to this day, I don't believe she knows how much that means to me. As I look back at the situation, I overcame me viewing Sarah as one of my biggest enemies; to Sarah now becoming one of my biggest advocates. She's my mom "away" from my mom. If Billie Renee is my first heartbeat, Sarah is my second. I love her dearly, and I know she knows that.

Black Magic
Artist: Styles P (Ft. Angie Stone)
Album: A Gangster and a Gentlemen

Although the incident had occurred between Sarah and myself, I had to immediately switch mental gears in preparation for my upcoming first year of middle school. I had just finished my tenure at Southern Hills, and graduated elementary school as one of the top students in my fifth-grade class, and in order to continue my educational progression, my mother set up the opportunity for me to test for entry into Caddo Middle Magnet School.

"Nicholas, this is a very important test you have to take tomorrow," my mother said.

"Ok, momma."

"I'm serious Nicholas. I need you to focus and do well so that you can get into this school."

"Ok...Ok...momma!"

My mother only pressured me to do extremely well in school. She knew that education was a key tenant to success, and the chance to attend Caddo Middle Magnet School would assist in accelerating my opportunities for a successful future.

She went to Barnes and Nobles Bookstore to buy some Math and English tutorial books, like those that prepared a student for the SAT or ACT. I began studying them multiple weeks prior to my fifth-grade school year ending, up until the night before the test. I felt as though I was prepared, but my anxiousness wouldn't allow me to sleep the night before I took the exam. I had so much running through my head.

"What if I flunked the test," I thought. "Would my mom be mad?"

"The test is supposed to be 4 hours," I recalled my mom telling me. "What in the hell could we be testing on for 4 hours," I pondered.

Fresh out of my altercation with Sarah, I began to think "I wonder if Sarah is still mad at me...what's my dad thinking?"

I was mentally drained with all these thoughts running through my head. I just wanted tomorrow morning to come and go. Hopefully, I would come out victorious, but if I didn't, I'd have to make the best out of every situation, just as my mom and I always had done. I got in bed and relaxed with my hand behind my head as I stared at the ceiling, eventually falling asleep to the tunes of my radio playing in the background.

I woke up the next morning to the smells of bacon, eggs, and biscuits. I marched down to the kitchen and see my mom whipping up some eggs.

"Go on and sit down at the table baby. It's time to eat."

"Yes ma'am," I replied as I sat at our dining room table. My mom brought out a plate filled with everything she had cooked. I began to eat, then I started to get up to go to my room.

"Where are you going," said my mom.

"To get my math book."

"Boy, sit down and eat. If you don't know it now, these ten minutes aren't going to do anything to change that."

"Yes ma'am," I replied.

"Nicholas," my mom said, as she looked me in my eyes. "Relax...you're going to do just fine. Just do what you've always done and you'll have no worries."

I nodded my head in agreement and finished up my breakfast before heading off to my room to change clothes.

We load into the car and drive to Caddo Middle Magnet School to take the test.

As we reach the school, my mom parks her car in a near empty parking lot in front of this monstrous building.

"Momma," I inquired in amazement. "This is the school?"

"Sure is. Let's go!"

We head out the car and follow the signs through the front entrance that lead to the testing room where the female test administrator welcomed us. We were the first family to arrive.

"Hello," she said. "Are you here to take the entrance exam?"

"Yes Ma'am."

"What's your name?"

"Nicholas Battle."

"Ma'am," the administrator now signals to my mom. "Do you have any identification for him?"

"Yes," replies my mom as she pulls out my elementary school ID card and birth certificate.

"Ok, Mr. Battle. You can sit at chair number three."

I walk to my chair and sit down. My mom remained

standing at the door and silently mouthed, "Good luck…I love you" before she exited the room.

Eventually, more students began to fill the room. As I look around, I noticed that there was only one other black kid taking the exam. As if we had known each other for years, we nodded our heads at each other in acknowledgement. I was anxious to begin the test, but more ready for it to be over once the realization had set in that I would be in the room until 2PM. I released a nervous sigh before the test administrator stood in the front of the room and began handing out the test and giving instructions.

"The test will begin at 10AM promptly," she stated as she individually placed the tests on everyone's desks. "It is a multiple-choice exam that requires you to fill in the circle of the correct answer with a #2 pencil, of which you have two already on your desk."

"If you need a new sharpened pencil, raise your hand and I'll bring you another one. Are there any questions?"

Silence within a full classroom of eleven-year old kids was a nod of agreement. The timer started and the test began. The four hours seemed like an eternity, but at last, we finished. I walked outside, where my mom greeted me.

"How'd you do?"

"I think I did good."

"Well, that's good."

"Yes ma'am," I replied. "The test lady said the scores would go out in two weeks."

"I think you'll be fine baby," said my mom in a reassuring voice. "To celebrate, where do you want to go?"

"Can we go to Ryan's," I replied.

"Let's go, my Magnet School boy!"

"Momma," I replied. "Don't jinx it!"

My mom begins to chuckle at my response as we head to the car. We go out to eat and then go back home. I felt relieved that the test was over. Now, I had to get through these next two weeks of waiting to see if acceptance or not into the school could happen. Thankfully, the testing portion was all wrapped up.

Our daily mail delivery came to our apartment everyday around noon. After about a week of negotiating, I convinced my mom to let me have the mail key so that I could check to see if my results had come in. On the Monday at the start of week two, I check the mail...nothing from the school. The same went for Tuesday and Wednesday; however, on

Thursday, a white envelope, addressed to my mom from the Caddo Middle Magnet School had arrived. I grabbed it and ran to the house. I picked up the phone and began calling my mom at work.

"Good afternoon, this is Billie."

"Momma," I replied in excitement.

"Hey baby, what you got going on?"

"The letter came!"

"The school letter?"

"Yessss!"

"Well, did you open it yet?"

"No ma'am," I replied. "Not yet!"

"Well open it!"

"Ok."

I tear the top off the envelope and pull out the tri-folded piece of paper. I unfolded it and began to read the memo to my mom over the phone.

"Dear Ms. Battle," I began to read. "It is my pleasure to inform you that your child, Nicholas Battle, is accepted for admission into Caddo Middle Magnet..."

"Momma," I paused. "I made it!"

"Yes, you did baby," she replied.

I could hear the joy in my mom's voice. She may have been more excited for me than I was. My mom always wanted me to have a better life than she had, and although we never had much, she continually placed me in opportunities to gain a greater academic knowledgebase than what she attained. To see her son could excel in places that she was not privy to, excited her and validated that she was doing everything possible to propel me to having the access to resources necessary for me to achieve a bright future. She now enjoyed seeing me achieve everything she dreamed of accomplishing throughout her life. I relished in giving her that excitement. She was a proud mom; however, I too was a proud son.

The Light
Artist: Common
Album: Like Water for Chocolate

My sixth-grade school year had finally started and since my acceptance into Caddo Middle Magnet, a school bus picked me up and dropped off the children who attended the school. No longer did my mom have to wake up extremely early to bring me to school, or leave work early to come and pick me up, as she had to at Southern Hills Elementary. I was just happy that I was my own little "man" and becoming more self-sufficient.

Every morning, I would walk to the apartment complex entrance and wait for my bus to come. While waiting, I would bring my cassette tape player and listen to music to begin my day. Music was like my coffee at that time. It was my jolt of caffeine to get me going. This new group by the name of "Bone Thugs-N-Harmony" had just came out with a new single called "Thuggish Ruggish Bone." At that time, I didn't know what the hell the title of the song meant, but the intro to the song felt like it was tailor-made for a young black male, like myself, attending a majority white populated Caddo Middle Magnet School.

"We're not against rap. We're not against rappers. But we are against those thugs," is what the intro to the song said. My middle school was comprised of only 10 – 15% blacks; therefore, while in a class, there might only be one or two blacks out of an entire 25-person class. There were many snide comments made by some of the white students.

"They'll let anybody in here," whispered one kid in my chemistry class.

I had a temper, but my mom had previously briefed me that I could not get in any trouble at this school. This was my best school option in Shreveport, so I had to be the "bigger" man in situations like that.

Instead of reacting to the few hateful comments I received, I "showed up" my classmates by outperforming them. I made sure I aced everything I did in all my classes. I sat in one of the front desks of every class I was in and answered every question asked of the teacher. Nobody was going to question whether I deserved to be here.

I would reflect upon the struggles it took for me to get where I was.

"Fuck it," I would think to myself. "Yes, grew up in Motown and Queensborough, but I'm no lesser of a student than anyone in this school."

If I give it my all, my 100% will best any other student's 100% any day of the week. I was smart. I was confident. But, moreover, I was just as worthy as anybody else to succeed. Some may have just viewed my outer shell and thought differently of what I could bring to this school; however, they were in for a rude awakening when they saw my work ethic. Plus, when I finished busting your ass in the classroom, I was going to my locker between classes to grab my Walkman and headphones to listen to music that reflected my Motown and QB roots.

Monday may have been a constant repeat of Thug Life's "Bury Me a G" single, followed by "How Long Will They Mourn Me." Tuesday was Warren G's "Do You See" and "This is the Shack." Wednesday was Outkast's complete *Southernplayalisticcadillackmuzik* album, while Thursday was UGK's "Front, Back, & Side to Side". I always finished Friday off with one of the most clever and creative pieces of work ever created; Nas' *Illmatic* album.

No matter what, I was not going to abandon my culture because of my surroundings. I'm an 80's baby, meaning Hip-Hop ran through my veins. It fueled me through studying for tests. It gave me a mental edge over my classmates. It propelled me to another straight 'A' school year. Hip Hop was my outlet.

BATTLE'S BLUEPRINT

Unorganized chaos results in detrimental conflict. Detrimental conflict results in negative profit margins.

Through this school year, my mom continued to date Larry. It had been over a year now, and he had become a constant piece of our unit. As before, Larry would come to Shreveport every other week, or so, and just fit into our routine so easy. By this time, everyone had met him; from my grandma Vergie, to my grandma Mattie and my PawPaw. They all loved him, no matter what color he was. If he treated my mom and me with the utmost respect, everything was all good in everyone's eyes.

Larry loved music also. He was more R&B and old-school; however, if the beat was nice and lyrics were on point, he'd listen to some rap too. He had since gotten rid of his SS Monte Carlo and bought a Chevy Lumina. He and I were driving one weekend to get some lunch while my mom was out shopping. Method Man and Mary J Blige's single "You're All I Need" came on.

"Aww man," I said. "Larry, turn that up...that's my

joint!"

"Cool," he replied as he turned up the volume.

"I like that one buddy," Larry said. "Who is that?"

"Method Man and Mary J. Blige!"

"Is that Aretha Franklin sampled in the background?"

"Larry," I replied with a sarcastic look on my face. "You sure you ain't black man?"

We both laugh before Larry turns down the music a little bit.

"Hey buddy," he said. "I gotta ask you something man."

"What's up?"

"You know I love your mom, right?"

"Uhhh…yea."

"Well, you know I fell in love with you first. I love you buddy."

I didn't know how to react at this moment. It was the first time a male figure in my life had expressed their love for me through saying those three words, and not just through actions. I didn't know if I knew what "love" was outside of the "love" I received from my immediate family, but Larry was like family now, so I replied.

"I love you too, man."

"So…uhhh…how would you feel if your mom and I got married?"

"Uhh…I don't know," I said in a shocked voice.

"Well, I want your blessings first before I ask her. That's how much I love you."

I sat and thought about what Larry had just said. This was a huge moment, but after I slight pause, I relayed my thoughts on the situation.

"Mom loves you…I can tell. You marrying her is cool with me, man! I think she'd say yes!"

Larry looked at me with a smile resembling a sigh of relief over his face. I was glad he was going to ask my mom to marry him. Selfishly, I didn't want to relinquish my "man of the house" duties, but for Larry, I'd make an exception.

TRACK #6: SO MANY TEARS

Artist: 2Pac
Album: Me Against the World

What made Pac different than any other artist is that his music remains relevant, to this day. His music is timeless…like a Van Gogh or Michelangelo piece of art. He was real and authentic.

Through this time in my life, I shed so many mental tears and it was emotionally draining. Life was never the same from this point on.

My mom and Larry got married a couple of months before I finished my sixth-grade school year. Although I was excited for their union, I was hesitant to leave Shreveport, especially me leaving the presence of the only father-figure I had known...my PawPaw. Larry was in the Army and stationed in Fort Hood, so by the end of the school year, we were set to move to Killeen, Texas

It was the necessary time for us to leave Shreveport. Regardless of if my mom got married or not, she would always tell me to not get too comfortable living in Shreveport because, by the time I reached high school, we would not be there.

My mom had an ultimate plan to get us out of our current situation. Ever since we got our own apartment, my mom would put away a little money each month in hopes of saving enough funds to secure a down payment on a house. Although Shreveport would not be my mom's desired final location, she wasn't going to move too far from our family though. She looked at areas such as Keithville or Mansfield, Louisiana; areas between 30 to 45 minutes away from our current location. I could handle this distance; however, a six-hour drive to Killeen was not a distance that would be applicable for me to travel and see my grandparents on a frequent basis. For my first time ever, I feared losing my family. I was terrified that my life would never be the same.

As the school year came to an end, my eagerness to move to Texas became a restlessness turmoil of emotions. I never envisioned living life without seeing my grandparents on a weekly basis, especially my PawPaw. Not only was he a grandparent, he was my surrogate father, my best friend, and my everything. Leaving was going to be difficult and I wasn't ready for it, but the morning for our travels to Texas had finally come about.

It was time for us to get in my mom's car and drive to Texas. We drove to my Grandma Vergie's house to say our goodbyes, followed by my Grandma Mattie and PawPaw's house. As we come pull into the driveway, I noticed my PawPaw's van was not home yet, but we parked anyway and made our way to the front door. My grandma always kept the front door open because of the glass-screened door that sat in front of it. She was sitting at the kitchen table when we came to the door.

"Hey there," my grandma said as she opened the door.

"Hey grandma," I replied.

"Hey Ms. Brown," replied my mom.

"So, you guys are going to hit the road now," my grandma said in a somber voice.

"Yes ma'am," replied my mom. "It's gonna be a long drive."

"Yes, indeed it will," said grandma. "Renee…let us keep Nicholas while you go down to Texas."

My eyes perked up as I heard her say that, as I didn't want to leave Shreveport. My focus and attention now shifted towards my mom.

"Ms. Brown, you know I can't leave my baby."

"I know. We're just going to miss him sooo much."

Hearing my mom's response brought the move to Texas into a greater reality. To avoid tearing up, I changed the subject in a hurry.

"Grandma, where is PawPaw?"

"You and your PawPaw boy," she replied. "He's at work baby. He won't be back for another 30 minutes or so."

"Ok."

"Well, Ms. Brown," replied my mom. "We gotta go and see David before we leave too. I hate Mr. Brown is not here.

I'll make sure we call over here before we leave David's and hit the road."

"Ok sweetie."

We exit the house and get into the car. My grandma closed the door behind us and stood in front of the door and watched the car as we pulled away from the house. As we turn to drive down the Francis Street, my mom honks the horn and we begin our final drive through Shreveport to go see my Uncle David.

The reality of leaving was beginning to hit my chest like a hammer hits a nail head.   My emotions became uncontrollable as a few tears began to stream down my face. I quickly turned my head and dried my face so my mom wouldn't see my cry. We finally make it to my Uncle David's house and get out the car as he greets us at the front door.

"What's up my people!"

"Hey Unc," I replied, still holding back tears.

We walk into the house and my mom talks to my uncle for a while before she decides it's time to leave.

"Nicholas," said my mom. "Call your PawPaw before we leave."

"Ok," I replied as I grabbed the phone and dialed my

grandparent's house.

"Hello," answered my grandma.

"Hey grandma," I replied. "We're at David's house and about to leave."

"Ok," she sadly stated. "You wanna talk to PawPaw?"

"Yes ma'am."

"Earl," my grandma said to PawPaw. "Nicholas is on the phone."

"Hey Shotgun," PawPaw said with a crackling voice. "Are y'all about to leave?"

"Yes sir," I replied as tears began streaming down my face.

"Ok," said PawPaw as he now began to cry. "PawPaw loves you."

"I love you too."

BATTLE'S BLUEPRINT
You must learn to become "comfortable" being "uncomfortable." When life throws you a challenge, you must strive to overcome the obstacles presented to you.

I hung up the phone, continuing to cry as if I was never

going to see my PawPaw again. My uncle David gave me a hug and reassured that everything was going to be ok. My mom and I get into the car and proceed to the highway, as I remained crying. With every mile we distanced ourselves from Motown, my tears increased exponentially. By the time we reached the Texas state highway marker, I had cried myself to sleep. When I woke up, we were 30 minutes away from our new home. Our new life was about to begin and I didn't know how I felt about it. Only time would tell.

A New Day Begins
Artist: Cormega
Album: Mega Philosophy

Our living situation in Killeen was far different than what we were accustomed to in Shreveport. We now had a four-bedroom house, that we owned. There was no more apartment living with neighbors above and beside us. We had a nice sized front yard and fenced-in backyard. Our neighbors were welcoming and seemed to enjoy us. It was like we had achieved the American dream, although I still would rather be in Shreveport at this time.

We had settled in Killeen for a couple of weeks now. It was the summer time and I was in a foreign location with no friends or family around me. Larry could tell that I wasn't adapting to Texas as well as he would have hoped I would, so he figured he'd do something nice for me easing my transition.

"Nicholas."

"Yes."

"Go in the garage and get that basket of clothes off of the washer for me please."

"Ok," I replied as I proceed to the garage. I opened the door and saw a brand new 10-speed mountain bike resting on its kickstand. I look back at Larry with a look of awe on my face.

"Hey buddy," Larry said with a slight grin on his face. "Go riding and have some fun man. Matter of fact, why don't you go ride up to see your new school."

"Ok...Cool man," I said with the first glimpse of excitement I had since I left Shreveport. I grabbed my Walkman and hopped onto my new bike to ride to Palo Alto Middle School, my new school I'd be attending.

As I rode up hill on Westrim Drive in the Willow Springs neighborhood, I popped in my new tape I got from Circuit City by the Long Beach California group, "The Dove Shack." As I pass a few houses and get to the school, "Summertime in the LBC" begins to play. Instead of singing "LBC," I replaced it with "Willow Springs."

"Summertime in the Willow Springs," I sang and laughed. This was the first time I felt comfortable in my new surroundings. It was the first time I felt secure

As I rode my new "toy" home, I saw my mom pulling her car in the garage. I tapped my brakes, dismounted my bike, and walked it into the garage.

"I see you're riding your new wheels," said my mom.

"Yea! Thanks mom!"

"Glad you like it…You deserve it."

We both walk into the house, and for the first time while living in Killeen, I felt like we were a family. Mom and Larry were on board; however, my resistance was the only thing holding us back from becoming a complete unit. Everything felt right now. I was all in.

NINOSCORNER

Hypnotized (on) Cash Money
Artist: Tear Da Club Up Thugs (Ft The Hot Boys & Baby)
Album: CrazyNDaLazDayz

Living in a house is completely different than the apartment life I knew. Our living space was larger; therefore, as our house size increased, the amount of cleaning to keep the house organized increased. Additionally, Larry liked our yard to be one of the better-looking ones on our street, so as my household duties regressed from being the "man" of the house to the "son," to me being the designated yard-hand.

Cutting yards should be an easy task I thought; however, there were rules to this in our household.

"Nicholas," shouted Larry. "Come to the living room."

I scurried to the living room from my bedroom to see what Larry wanted.

"Starting tomorrow, you're the yardman of the house."

"Ok," I said with an uneasy look on my face, since I had never cut a yard before in my life.

"Don't worry, it's easy peazy buddy," replied Larry. "I'll show you how to do everything in the morning."

"Ok."

"Now once you get everything down pat, there's a few things I expect of you."

"Ok."

"One…I need you to cut the yard once a week…every week."

"Ok."

"Two…You gotta fertilize the yard every three months and over-seed the yard with it…Got it?"

"What's over-seed?"

"Basically, put down more grass seed after you fertilize and water the yard."

"Ohhh."

"The fertilizer keeps the grass green and the extra seed makes the grass in the yard thicker and healthier."

"Got it!"

"And number three…before the fall and winter seasons start, I need you to put down some winter rye grass seed."

"Is that the same as over-seeding," I replied.

"Not necessarily," said Larry. "It's grass seed that you plant before it gets cold that keeps the grass thick and green all year round."

"Cool!"

"You'll get $10 a week to do all this…ok?"

"Sounds good to me," I replied as I went back into my room to get ready for bed as it was late in the evening. That $10 sounded good to me, so I was ready to see what this yard cutting "thing" was all about.

The next morning, I put on some old sweat pants and a t-shirt to get ready for the yard work. Larry was in the kitchen, fixing a cup of coffee. I sat down and ate a bowl of cereal before we went outside so that Larry could show me how to operate the lawn mower.

"Nicholas, first off, you have to make sure the lawn mower has gas in its tank. Once you've done that, you prime the mower by pressing this button three or four times."

"What's prime?"

"When you prime a lawnmower, you're putting gas into the lawn mower carburetor to help it start the engine."

"Why," I replied.

"Well, when the lawnmower sits for a while, the gas that rests in the gas line usually evaporates after a period of time."

"Oh," I replied. "I get it. So, once you prime it, then the gas goes back in the line to help start the mower?"

"Yep...you got it. And, to start the lawnmower, just pull that cord on the side until the motor turns over."

I pulled the cord, and on my first try, the lawn mower started. Larry told me to turn it off and gave me a brief tutorial on how to work the weed eater and edger. It seemed straight forward, so I started the lawn mower again and got to work as Larry went back inside.

I mowed the yard to perfection. Not one sliver of grass missed my mower's blades. Nothing went uncut in both the front and backyard. The front yard trimming along the sidewalk looked so good that you would have thought a barber had come down to give it a razor-tight edge. It was beautiful. I stood back and looked at the yard in admiration of my work. I was proud of my accomplishment.

"Larry," I said as I walked back into the house. "I'm finished."

"Ok," replied Larry as he got up from the kitchen table and walked outside to look at my work. He examined the whole yard. He walked around the front yard and nodded his head in satisfaction at what he was looking at.

"Looks good buddy," he said. "Let's go check out the backyard."

We head to the back. He examines the fence line to make sure no weeds are on the fence. He checked the side of the house making sure I removed all the grass trimmings sprouting from the slab edges.

"Really good," Larry repeats as we both walk inside the house, as the day was beginning to get hotter. He hands me a crisp $10 for my services and I accepted it in excitement.

"Thank you," I said with a grin on my face.

"You earned it buddy."

The wheels began to start turning in my head as I realized how easy that $10 was to make.

"Larry," I stated. "How much is a normal yard cut around here?"

"I've seen most advertised at $25 a mow for every two weeks of service."

"So, basically, we're talking about $50 per month or $12.50 a week these people budget around here," I pondered.

"Yep," replied Larry. "Sounds about right."

"If I can get the chance to cut a few yards in the neighborhood, can I use the lawnmower, edger, and weed-eater?"

"Yea," replied Larry. "As long as you make the lawnmower your own responsibility. You must keep it gassed up. You have to keep it tuned up, and you have to change the oil in it too."

"Cool!"

"And," Larry continued, "You have to keep the blade sharpened. The lawn equipment will be all your responsibility if you want to do this."

I thought about it for a minute. I never really had anything that I owned. My only previous responsibility was keeping our Shreveport apartment clean before my mom came home from work. Taking on this obligation was a risk that I had never thought about having; however, after a moment of thought, I had made my decision.

"Alright Larry, I think I want to do this," I replied. "Maybe I can save enough money to buy my own car when I turn 16."

"Well, let's make a deal," Larry responded to me. "However, much money you have in the bank when you turn 16, your mother and I will double it so that you can get your first car."

"Really?!"

"Yep."

BATTLE'S BLUEPRINT
Do not live in the moment. Discover your talent and invest in your craft.

I immediately started thinking about getting my newfound business off the ground. How would I get the word out? How much would I charge per yard? What parts of the neighborhood would I target?

As I glanced to the left of me, I saw my mom sitting on the couch as a lightbulb clicked in my head.

"Momma, can you print me off some flyers from your job?"

"I'm pretty sure I can…"

"Ok," I thought. "Can the flyer have my name at the top with 'Lawn Mower Service' underneath it…and our home phone number at the bottom?"

"Aren't you forgetting something," replied my mom.

"Ummmm…"

"The price boy!"

"Oh," I remembered. "Well, if the average person charges \$25 every other week, I think I'll go for \$20."

"Ok."

"Yea momma, I figure if I charge less than my competition, I can get more business."

"Well look at my little businessman!"

"Yes ma'am," I replied. "I gotta get this money!"

My mom chuckled as she began to make us some weekend lunch; chili cheese dogs and French fries. We ate lunch and followed it up with a few movies before nighttime had arrived. The weekend was near an end. I was in complete 'hustle' mode from this day forward. It was time to go *get* it.

The Monday following my business discussion with the family, my mom came home from work with my new flyers for my business.

"Nicholas," she yelled. "Come get these flyers!"

I ran to the living room to see my mom's creation. I pick up the folder with the flyers in it and begin to read it.

"Nick's Lawn Care," read the first line, followed by "$20 per yard" and our phone number on the last line.

"Momma," I said. "That looks dope! How many did you print?"

"A hundred."

I smiled with enjoyment. At that moment, I knew my summer plans were now set in motion. It was time to be my own boss and begin to make things happen.

The next morning, I awoke to an empty house. My mom and Larry both worked this morning. I made my bed up, groomed myself, and dressed before heading to the kitchen table to get the flyers my mom printed for me. With flyers in hand, I headed out the door.

I walked to the intersection of my street and began placing flyers in all the doors of the residents in our neighborhood. My street alone had 60 homes. I went over to our neighboring street, Paintrock Drive, and placed out the remaining 40 flyers. I was still around 20 flyers short of fulfilling my flyer "duties" on Paintrock Dr. I went home and called my mom, as I needed more flyers to complete my job.

"Scott and White Hospital, this is Billie."

"Momma…"

"Hey baby," she replied. "What's up?"

"Can you print out some more flyers for me…I ran out."

"Twenty more Nicholas," she whispered. "And then you have to ride your bike up to the store to make copies…ok?"

"Ok," I replied as my mom hung up the phone.

My mom came home on her lunch break and brought me the remaining flyers. I got on my bike and rode a few miles up the street to the shopping plaza in Willow Springs. I used the $10 I got for cutting our yard to make copies of the flyer. At $0.05 per copy, I was able to get another 100 copies for $5.

I received my copies and rode my bike back to my neighborhood. I finished off the flyers on a few of my neighboring streets and went back home. Now, all I could do is wait to see if anyone would give me a chance to earn their business.

Every day without an inquiry for lawn service seemed like an eternity. Wednesday passed with no call. Thursday flew by with the same result. Friday was near an end before the phone rang. I heard Larry answer the phone.

"Hello?"

"Hello," answered a woman with a strong Asian dialect.

"I'm calling in reference to the lawn service."

"Ok," replied Larry. "That's my son's company. Let me get him for you."

Larry walked to the room and handed me the phone.

"Hello," I answered.

"Yes sir, I would like to request your lawn service," replied the lady. "When are you available?"

"I can come by tomorrow morning if that's fine with you?"

"Yes, that will work."

"I'll see you at 9AM. And what is your name ma'am?"

"Jun."

"Alright Ms. Jun, I'll be there promptly in the morning."

Ms. Jun gave me her address as we finished our phone call. I walked into the living room to tell my mom and Larry that I had secured my first client.

"Cha-Ching," I spouted with a laugh. "First customer booked!"

"Well, well...lookey here," replied mom. "Congrats baby!"

"Thanks mom!"

"Congrats buddy!"

"Thanks Larry!"

I walked into my room that night with a huge grin on my face. I was excited for the opportunity, but more excited to start earning some money to get my first car in a few years.

"Larry done fucked up," I mumbled to myself. "I'm bout to get this money…and this car," I said to myself as I fell asleep with a smile on my face. The hustle was about to begin.

I woke up the next morning with an eagerness that I haven't felt in a while. After grooming myself, I put on some old sweat pants and a t-shirt before heading to the kitchen. I threw on some old tennis shoes and grabbed a bottle of water from the refrigerator as I walked out the kitchen door into the garage. I draped my weed-eater, broom, and edger over my lawnmower as I began my walk to Ms. Jun's house. Her house was just a few blocks up the street, so it didn't take me long to arrive. I get to her house and park my lawn equipment in her front yard, as I walked to her front door to ring the doorbell. As the door opened, my jaw almost dropped. Ms. Jun was fine as hell; something like 'Ms. Parker' from the movie 'Friday.' She was a shorter Korean woman with a bobbed cut hair style. She came to the door in tight jeans, open-toed sandals, and a form fitting shirt that revealed her augmented accessories.

"Hello…how are you doing," said Ms. Jun in her native accent.

"Uhhh…yes ma'am," I said as I tried to keep my eyes 'up.' "I'm Nick Battle…here to cut your lawn."

"Oh…ok," she replied. "You're much younger than I thought you'd be. How old are you?"

"Twelve."

"Just a baby," she grinned. "Follow me around the house so I can show you what needs to be cut."

I followed Ms. Jun around the house. She wanted the full front and backyard cut, just like I did at home, with a normal edge and weed eat. It was nothing spectacular, but it was my first job. It had to be perfect.

"Yes ma'am, I can do this for you…shouldn't take me more than an hour and a half."

"Ok," she replied. "Just knock on the door when you finish."

"Yes ma'am," I said as Ms. Jun walked back into her house, with my eyes following her.

I walked back to the front yard to start the job. I did everything Ms. Jun asked, and like clockwork, I went to her door 90 minutes later to let her know I finished.

"You're done already…"

"Yes ma'am."

"Come on, let's walk around and take a look," she replies as we do a scope of her yard. We walked throughout the front and back and she nodded in acceptance of the work I had done.

"Good job," she says as she hands me two folded over bills.

"Ms. Jun, you handed me $25…I only charge $20."

"The extra is for your tip," she replied. "Can you come by every other week?"

"Yes ma'am!"

"Good…I'll see you in two weeks."

I left Ms. Jun's house with a sense of pride and accomplishment. Essentially, I just began my self-owned business, even though my roster of clients was a full list of only Ms. Jun.

Doin' My Job
Artist: T.I.
Album: Trap Muzik

Over the next two weeks, I received six more calls for my lawn services, with four becoming recurring customers. Two of those new recurring customers were a direct referral from Ms. Jun.

I now had 5 steady customers, meaning 10 total yards to cut per month; netting me $200 per month from my lawn business. My rule of thumb was to deposit my earnings from 8 of the 10 yards in the bank. The remaining 2 yards, plus any tips, would be money for me to enjoy the fruits of my labor with. The work was tiring but the money was worth it. Although I didn't turn 16 for another 3 and a half years, I was determined to save enough money for my first vehicle.

As the summer ended and my 7th grade school year approached, I had saved nearly $350 in my bank account. I wasn't going to become a millionaire from cutting yards, but I realized real soon that my first job was going to be a slow and steady grind to reach my desired goal.

Since Texas stayed hot nearly all year round, I was able to continue my lawn business into the month of October. By the end of my first lawn season, I was able to save almost $800.

Larry was a huge car fan, and always brought car buying magazines to the house. I sat on the living room couch and began to read one, as Larry walked in from his bedroom.

"What you reading buddy?"

"Looking at cars…"

"Cars," he replied. "What kind are you looking at?"

"I don't know…something between 5 or 6 grand."

"5 or 6 grand?!" Larry questioned.

"Yep," I continued. "I figure I'll have at least 3 grand saved up before I turn 16. And when y'all double it, I can work with that!"

"Damn," Larry mumbled. "I created a monster!"

The school year went as every other year previously went. I performed well. In fact, school was now on auto-pilot, as I felt extremely prepared due to the foundation, I received from Caddo Middle Magnet in Shreveport. The only thing I worried about now was the start of lawn season; and in Texas, that meant around March.

As my second lawn season approached, I expanded my

business. I printed out another 200 flyers and placed them in neighborhoods I did not service in the previous season. I was able to gain four more yards, to my normal rotation, bringing my total count to 9 recurring customers.

I was bringing in nearly $400 per month from my business. I always paid myself first, meaning a set minimum percentage of my funds went to my bank account before I ever enjoyed my additional spending change. I was now stocking away $300 a month into my account, totaling $900 to start the lawn season, and $1,700 overall. I was only 13 years old, with the mindset of a seasoned businessman. I had a goal in sight, and I wasn't going to deviate from my plan.

Where Have You Been
Artist: Jay-Z (Ft. Beanie Sigel)
Album: The Dynasty – Roc La Familia

It was the end of the school year and my lawn business was flourishing; however, since it was the start of the summer, it was time for me to visit my dad, Sarah, and my sister for a couple of weeks. My dad called once school ended and said he'd be in Killeen the upcoming Monday to pick me up to come to Dallas. It would be the first time I had come back to Dallas after the incident that occurred between my stepmom and myself. I was a little uneasy at first; however, this was something we would all have to eventually get past, so we might as well start the healing process now.

Monday morning had come and my dad had reached our house in Killeen. My mom and Larry were at work, so I called them both to let them know my dad had arrived and I was on my way to Dallas with him. I loaded my suitcase in the back of my dad's black Mazda truck before we pulled out of the driveway to head to his house. We converse in small-talk until we reached Waco, Texas; about the midway point between Killeen and Dallas. My dad became silent before getting the courage to being speaking again.

"Nicholas," my dad hesitantly stated. "I got something to tell you."

"What's up dad?"

"When we get to Dallas, we're going to be going to church tonight."

"Ok," I replied. "That's all? We go to church on Sundays, but if Mondays is your thing, that's cool."

"Naw," my dad responded. "We're going to a rehab meeting at the church."

"Rehab?"

"Yea, because of my recent battle with drugs."

I looked down towards the floor of my dad's truck. I was speechless and had no idea of what to say.

"Drugs," I thought silently to myself. "What the fuck?"

I was shocked that my dad had succumb to drugs, especially knowing exactly how my grandparents felt about the topic. Their house was a "drug-free" zone; therefore, I thought the environment in which my dad grew up in would deter him from even thinking about attempting any foreign substance.

In a sad, but disappointed manner, I began to continue the dialogue with my dad.

"What kind of drugs dad?"

"Crack," he replied in a sketchy and embarrassed voice.

BATTLE'S BLUEPRINT

Do not only share your successes. Be transparent and share your failures as well. The key to not repeating history is to learn from it.

I was motionless and silent. My eyelids became heavy, as I wanted to cry, but didn't want to show an extreme case of emotions in front of my dad. My throat began to feel heavy as well, suggesting that if I were to begin talking, no words would exit my mouth…only a weep that would eventually lead to crying. I had to stay strong though; not just for myself, but mostly for my dad. If I were to break down, how would he react to that?

"You alright," said my dad.

"Yea," I said with a shaking voice. "Dad," I responded. "Why?"

"I don't know…it was just something that happened…something that I wish never happened."

We sat silently for a few minutes. I could only imagine the thoughts that were going through my dad's head, because as his child, my mind was racing.

"Does grandma and PawPaw know?"

"Yea, they know."

"Ok," I replied. "Dad, are you done with it?"

"Yea, man…I'm done with that," he responded.

"Nicholas, if you don't listen to anything I ever say, just listen to this. Don't ever try that shit…ok?"

"Ok," I said. "But dad, how…how did you start doing it?"

"Well, I smoked weed and someone put crack in it without me knowing."

"Oh," I surprisingly replied.

Surprised, not because my dad smoked weed, and eventually smoked crack. Hell, from my previous visits to Dallas, I noticed the faint smell of weed on his clothes when he'd come into the house from work. I was more shocked that my dad let his guard down to the point where he was susceptible to a risk of this nature, especially considering the way my grandfather raised me. If he raised me this way, I'm quite sure my dad had the same teachings.

One of my PawPaw's lessons that he passed down to me was to never leave your drink unattended. If you leave the room and your drink doesn't leave with you, leave the drink where it is and go buy another one. As I remembered this piece of knowledge levied down on me from my PawPaw, I thought that my dad had to know the drink was the figurative language. It wasn't completely literal. If your drink could not be unattended, then surely your blunt couldn't either.

I looked at my dad in worried manner. I had just remembered that Sarah was pregnant with my little brother.

"Dad…dad…this won't affect the baby, will it?"

"No."

"But, what about crack babies," I responded.

"That's only if the mother is on drugs Nicholas."

"Oh, ok," I replied, still shocked at the information I had just received from my dad.

Seeing that I was still astonished, my dad began to reiterate his initial stance on the matter.

"Say man," he stated. "Don't ever fuck with that shit. It's nothing but trouble."

"Ok."

"Naw, I mean it Nicholas. It's nothing you ever want to experience, Ok?"

"Ok," I responded again as we continued our trip to Dallas. I stayed a little more than a week at my dad's house before returning home to Killeen. I enjoyed my time with my dad, Sarah, and my sister, but after the news I received concerning my dad, I had a lot to think about.

During my visit, all the feelings I had of yearning for the love of my dad was nearly nonexistent. I could not imagine the person whose attention I desired so much would surrender to the temptations of "crack."

I did a lot of soul searching and mental evaluations of myself after this trip. Before now, I wanted to walk like my dad…talk like my dad…shit, just be exactly my dad, especially since I always heard how much I was "like" my father. Not just how much I was like him, but how much I "acted" like him and exhibited some of his same character traits. After hearing of my dad's addiction, I wanted no parts of that comparison anymore. Honestly, he didn't deserve the opportunity for me to want to be like him.

I kept thinking how naive I was for paying so much homage and praise to a person who didn't do the same for me. As a youth, when I got in scuffles, my dad wasn't the man who taught me how to fight. That was my uncles David and John-John. When I wanted to learn how to ride my bike and get rid of my training wheels, my dad didn't teach me that. That was my mom. When I had football and baseball games, he didn't show up to see me play either. That was my mom and Larry. When I had parent-teacher lunch days in elementary school, my dad didn't come. My PawPaw did that.

When I looked back at life at that moment, I began to realize my dad never really did the little things for me or taught me shit. Hell, my mom was a young single parent, struggling to make it, and she never put him on child support. She never asked him for anything, and he never offered either.

When we had to start over from scratch after our apartment's looting by Bryant, there was no dad to console me and tell me everything would be alright. Those were some of my loneliest nights…ever. Nobody told my mom it was going to be "alright" but me. My role came by force to be the man of the house at an early age, but I can't be mad at that. It gave me the opportunity to learn at an early age, the pressure and pain it took to provide for a family.

When we moved to Killeen and the light finally shined over the dark period in our life, all the struggles my mom and I went through hardened us and became preparation for teaching us how to survive through any circumstance. Those same struggles made the fruits of our successes taste so much better.

From that moment on, I knew what to expect from my dad. Don't get me wrong, he was still my father and I loved him; however, I now realized that I made it this far in life due to my mom's hard work and diligent efforts. It was time for me to appreciate her a lot more, and not chase my dad for attention because, in all honesty, my mom deserved all the credit for my success…and that's without question.

Up to Me
Artist: Lil Wayne
Album: The Block is Hot

After arriving back in Killeen from my dad's house, I immediately went back to "grind" mode with my lawn service. I continued to save my money over the next couple of summers, and by now I had over $4,000 in the bank. I went from a skinny little kid that played video games daily, to a self-made entrepreneur, primed to purchase his first car within a few months.

I was finishing up my freshman year in high school at Ellison Ninth Grade Center with a 4.0 GPA. As the summer came, I was prepping myself for my vacation in Dallas with my dad and Sarah. The week after school ended, my dad picked me up from Killeen and we headed to his house. As we arrived, Sarah and the kids were in the living room watching TV. I went over to give them all a hug before bringing my suitcase to my room.

My sister, Carlena, was now 4 years old and my little brother, Dee, would turn 2 in November. It was always fun dealing with my siblings. Although we were only together for brief periods throughout the year, they were my heart. The moment I first laid eyes on them, I knew I had to be the "big brother" they needed. Every personal move I made was calculated. I just wanted to set a good example for them to follow. So, while I visited my dad during my summer breaks, I wanted to make sure that the bond between my siblings and I grew as strong as possible. I wanted them to know they had a brother they could always count on, no matter what, and the only way to do that was through presence and action.

During the visit, we didn't do too much. It was mostly relaxing at the house while my dad and Sarah went to work, while the kids went to daycare. It was a chill vacation. I was able to rest a little bit after finishing school, as well as take a small break from my lawn schedule.

On one Tuesday evening, my dad came home a little earlier than usual.

"Dad," I said. "You're home early. Where are the kids?"

"Sarah's gonna pick them up when she gets off."

"Oh…ok," I replied.

My dad immediately went into his bedroom on the backside of the house. He walked back out to the living room after a moment.

"Say man," my dad stammered. "Let your old man hold $20. I'll pay you back on Friday."

"Ok," I said with a confused tone in my voice. I reached in my back pocket to pull out my wallet and give my dad the money.

"Aight," he said as he walked to the front door. "I got you back on Friday."

"Ok…where are you going dad?"

"Uhhh…just to the store right quick," he replied in an uncertain manner.

"Aight," I replied as he left the house.

That was a weird moment for me. My mom never

borrowed money from me, and she raised me. To have my dad borrow money from me was absurd, in my opinion. He had a job and a wife who had a job also. He had a nice house and two nice vehicles. Was I missing something?

Maybe I was overthinking the situation. My dad could have simply forgot to get some cash out earlier in the week…or maybe, he mistakenly left his checkbook with my stepmom. There was no time for guessing anymore. There was no walking back my good deed. I would have to wait until Friday to see if my dad would hold his word.

Wednesday came and went, as did Thursday with no word from my dad on paying my money back. As I woke up on Friday morning, the house was empty. The parents were at work and the kids were at daycare. I had a lot of time to myself that day to think of a way to ask my dad for my money.

As the day progressed, I heard the front door knob shake as my dad opened the door and entered the house.

"Slick Nick," he said as he saw me sitting in the living room. "What's up?"

"Nothing much…just watching TV."

"Cool…cool," he responded as he walked to the kitchen

to get a soda.

I followed him into the kitchen and sat at the counter-height bar to continue to talk to my dad.

"Yo dad," I said. "You got that $20 for me?"

"Ohhhh, I forgot," he replied. "We're driving you home on next Friday after work. I got you then."

"Ok," I responded as I maintained my conversation with my dad throughout the remainder of the night.

The week flew by fast. Friday afternoon was here before I knew it. My dad and Sarah had made it home with the kids. My bags lay packed and posted at the door.

"Nicholas," yelled Sarah as she opened the door. "You ready?"

"Yes ma'am."

"Ok," Sarah replied as she went inside the house to freshen up.

I put my suitcase in the trunk of the car. My dad got my brother and sister situated in the car. Sarah went outside and put her purse in the front seat of the car. My dad and I stepped outside also. Sarah forgot something in the house and ran back inside for a quick moment. It was Friday, and my dad promised to get my money back to me today.

"Yo, dad," I said. "You got that $20 for me?"

"What? I got your God damned money…shit," he replied with an annoyed look on his face and an angry tone in his voice.

I was speechless. I didn't say anything else to my dad. I just got in the car and sat down in the back seat. Sarah came to the car and got in the passenger seat, as my dad got in the driver's seat. We backed out the driveway and made our way down the highway to Killeen.

BATTLE'S BLUEPRINT

Dissect the degrees of separation and understand who has your best interest in mind.

The entire three-hour ride home, I was completely silent. When my dad spoke to me, I responded in as minimal of words as possible. I couldn't believe my dad basically scolded me for asking for what was rightfully mine.

It wasn't about the small $20 "loan," it was the principle of the situation. I never asked my dad for a damn thing, even when times were hard, so why did he figure he had the right to ask me for money. To me, it was an insult. It made me feel as though he didn't care about my feelings or respect the fact that I worked hard for the money I saved. To say that he pissed me off was an understatement.

We arrived at my house in Killeen. I got out the car and said my goodbyes to Sarah and my siblings. My dad exited the car and got my suitcase out of the trunk. He took out a wrinkled ass $20 bill from his pocket and gave it to me before I went inside the house.

Was I glad that my dad gave me my money back? Yes. Was I mad at what events had to transpire for me to get my money back? Absolutely!

My dad walked me into my house and sat my suitcase in my mom's living room before saying his goodbyes and leaving. The distraught on my face was still evident from the situation that had occurred. My mom instantly noticed something wasn't right with me.

"Nicholas," she said. "Are you ok?"

"Yes ma'am."

"Are you sure?"

"Uhh…yes   ma'am,"   I   replied.   "But…my dad…ummm…my dad borrowed money from me and said he was going to pay me back a few days later."

"What!?!"

"Yes, and he didn't have the money when he said he was going to have it, so before we left to drive here today, I asked for my money."

"And….," replied my mom.

"He kinda cussed me out about getting my money back to me."

"You serious?"

"Yes ma'am," I responded. "But it was only $20."

"I don't give a damn if it was for a quarter," she replied.

"What in the hell makes him think he can borrow money from you," she continued to rant. "I ain't never ask his ass for shit regarding you! Now he has the nerve to take money from you!"

I just remained silent. I didn't know what to say. As my mom continued to unleash a barrage of comments about the situation, I quietly took my suitcase into my room and got in the bed. My anger remained, but my mom's furiousness at the situation boiled over. I laid in the bed and closed my door as my mom continued to vent to Larry about the incident. I fell asleep, just hoping that all this would blow over in the morning.

As I woke up Saturday morning, I heard the TV on in the living room. I got up and put my house-shoes on to go into the kitchen. Larry was sitting at the kitchen table drinking a cup of coffee. My mom had just walked in as well.

"Nicholas," my mom said to me. "Sit down at the able. I want to talk to you about something."

"Yes ma'am," I said as I sat down.

"The actions your dad pulled over on you this weekend absolutely pissed me off."

"Me too," I responded.

"Nobody, especially him, is going to use or take advantage of you…you understand?"

"I understand," I replied.

"He has never asked me if I needed help with you for anything. Since he wants to take money from you, I'm gonna make sure he'll never think of asking for money from you again."

"What do you mean momma?"

"I'm gonna put his ass on child support for these last 3 years of your high school," she responded. "But, if you don't want me to do it, I won't."

I thought hard about what my mom just told me. My initial thought was we've made it this far without any constant help from him, so why do we need it now? This was the best life I had ever experienced. My stepdad was set to retire from the military in a few months. My mom had a job making more money that she had ever made. We had two nice vehicles in the garage and owned our own house. We literally came from "nothing" to "something."

It wasn't about the money though. It was the principle. All I could think about was the anger my dad projected towards me over the inquiry concerning the money he borrowed from me, so in response, I replied with my answer.

"Momma," I responded. "It doesn't bother me at all. Do what has to be done."

BATTLE'S BLUEPRINT
Sometimes, you must make a hard decision even when you do not want to.

My mom nodded in agreement and we never spoke another word on the situation.

As selfish as it may have been, I wanted him to feel the

struggle my mom and I had to feel just a few years back. I didn't even feel bad over what transpired. In my eyes, he put himself in this predicament and he deserved it. He could have easily sent my mom a little money every month; however, he didn't choose that option.

My mom didn't have the luxury of whether to take care of me or not. She was essentially my mom and dad, wrapped into one person for much of my life, so the approximate $300 per month my dad had to pay over the next 3 years, was no comparison to the daily grind and sacrifices my mom went through to provide for me. It was chump change compared to what my mom dished out over the last 15 years of my life...chump change that he would be responsible for...for just 3 years. Honestly, he made out in the situation. Paying roughly $10,000 over 18 years for a kid is a steal...I'm just saying.

TRACK #7: TRIUMPH

Artist: Wu-Tang

Album: Wu-Tang Forever

I can still here O.D.B. yelling "Wu-Tang is forever" on this song. This group's efforts will never be recreated…9 dope artists who could murder a mic at any time when prompted to.

The Wu taught me that there is strength in numbers. So, as I strive for greatness and begin my Victory Lap (RIP Nip), it is mandatory that I educate my peers and future generations. It is necessary that I take them along for the ride, and eventually, let them take the wheel.

It was the summer of 1999. I had just finished my sophomore year of high school. I was maintaining a top 1% standing in my class, averaging a 4.2 GPA on a 4.0 scale. I saved more than $5,000 from mowing lawns to get my first car, and I was ready to go car shopping. Larry just walked into the house from work as I begin to think about what car I should buy.

"Hey Larry."

"What's up buddy?"

"Well," I said sarcastically, "when are we going to go car shopping?"

"Hmmmmmm...let's go tomorrow morning," he replied. "What kind of car do you want? A four door? A two door?"

"I think I want a four-door car," I responded.

"Ok, but better yet, let's go look right now."

"Really?" I responded.

"Yep...now come on!"

Larry and I hopped into his Chevy S-10 and drove down to the local car lot. As we got to the dealership, I saw a few cars that interested me. The first car I saw was a Canary

Yellow, 1995 Acura Integra GS-R. The sticker price was a little over $8,000.

"Larry," I said. "This is the one!"

"Um…no," he replied with a little laughter.

"Why not man?" I replied. "You said you'd double what I had in the bank when I turned 16 so I can get a car. I got over $5,000 saved up, so doubled, that would be $10,000. Instead of doubling that, just double $4,000 so I can get the car man…please?"

"Nicholas, you are 16 years old, and 9 times out of 10, you're going to get into some fender benders and accidents. Your first car will not be that expensive. Now, keep looking…"

"Well, what should my budget be?"

"$5,000 or under," said Larry.

"Ok."

I strolled through the car lot. The first car I saw in my price range was a 1991 Toyota Cressida for $4,999.

"How do you like this one?"

"Naw…I ain't feeling this one Larry."

The next vehicle I saw was a 1990 4-door Nissan Sentra

for $4,500.

"Not really feeling this one either Larry."

"Ok," responded Larry. "Just keep looking."

I walked down two more car aisles before seeing the car that would eventually call my name. It was an ocean-blue, 1992 Toyota Tercel. It was a 4-speed manual, with grey vinyl interior. The sticker price was $4,299.

"Larry," I said. "This is the one!"

"Oh, you like this one?"

"Oh yea!" I said with excitement.

"Ok, well let me take it for a test drive and check it over."

Larry took the car for a spin around the corner. He then brought the car back to the dealership and gave a thorough inspection of the engine and interior of the car.

"Nicholas, this is a really solid car. I like it too buddy."

"Me too!" I replied hastily. "Can we get it now?!"

"Pump the brakes man!" Larry replied laughing. "You know we gotta run this past momma first. If she agrees, then it's a done deal."

"Cool!"

Larry told the car dealer we'd be back tomorrow so that

my mother could see the car. He agreed to put a hold on the car for the next 24 hours prior to us leaving to go home.

When we arrived home, we told mom about the car, and she agreed to go see the car with us tomorrow. I went to bed that night more excited than ever. This was the moment a young 16-year old boy waited for…the opportunity to get his first car. What made it more special was that I had bust my ass for this car. Hopefully, I'd be pulling it off the car lot tomorrow afternoon.

As I woke up the next morning, I realized that today was the "day." I could be possibly buying my first car. I waited all day until my mom and Larry usually got home around 4PM. As the time came, Larry and my mom were a "no-show." Neither one had made it home yet. 5PM rolled around with no clue of where my parents were. My frustration built up because they weren't here. We were supposed to take mom to see the car. Plus, the dealership was only going to hold the car for 24 hours, which had just passed. "I'm screwed," so I thought.

As I walked to go sit at the kitchen table, I hear the garage door open.

"Finally!" I thought. "Now they want to come home!"

"Heyyy!" Says my mom as she opens the door.

"Hey…" I said non-enthusiastically.

"What's wrong with you?"

"Oh, nothing," I said in an unconvincing voice.

"Ok, well come outside and help me get these groceries out the car."

"Ok." I replied as I walked outside. I go to the garage and realize that my mom's car isn't in its normal spot. I thought that maybe it's outside, so I proceeded to the front yard. As I approached the driveway, I saw a welcome sight…an ocean blue 1992 Toyota Tercel, parked right behind Larry's Chevy truck.

"Momma…Larry!" I yelled. "Whattttt…haha…thank you…thank you…thank you!"

"It's yours baby!" My mom replied.

"Really?!"

"Yep," Larry confirms.

I was completely surprised by what Larry and mom did for me. Although, they had completely caught me off guard, I was grateful for the opportunity to have a car at 16. As I walk inside to the house, my mom yells out to me.

"Nicholas!"

"Yes ma'am..."

"You owe us $2,500 tomorrow..."

"Yes ma'am," I said with a chuckle. "I'll write you a check tonight!"

"You do that," my mom replied with laughter.

At that moment, the level of respect my parents had for me could not have been any higher. I was able to work hard to achieve something that I truly wanted, while still maintaining my academic standings throughout high school. Although I know Larry and my mom were always proud of me, they now fully knew that I understood the importance of: 1) the value of education 2) the value of money and 3) the value of time. All the life lessons they taught me were now shaping me into the man I would become.

Dear Mama
Artist: 2Pac
Album: Me Against the World

Growing up, I always realized how much my mom sacrificed for me to have better opportunities in life. She negotiated my spot into an elementary school outside my district and rarely bought herself nice things because she wanted to assure that I had the best. My mother devoted every spare second of her time to my extracurricular activities to make sure I stayed away from the temptations of the streets. She gave up her own life to assure mine would be better than what she had.

My mom had done so much for me as a youth, that I did not want her to worry about providing anything else for me. I made it my mission to be as self-sufficient as possible. That's the reason I started my own lawn business at the age of 12. It's also the same reason I worked at both McDonalds and Target while I was in high school.

Once I got my car, I made sure I never asked my mom or Larry for anything pertaining to my vehicle. Not only did I pay for my own maintenance on my car, I also paid my own car insurance. I just wanted to assure that my mom understood that I appreciated everything she had done for me. For that reason, I always strived to never disappoint her, and if I did, I felt as if I had failed as a son.

Since my mother had to relinquish her opportunity to go to college immediately after high school because of me, I felt it was my duty to attend college for the both of us. I promised myself that I would find a way to pay for my college also, so that my mom wouldn't have to worry about that either. Whether it be through loans or scholarships, I was determined to make this happen.

During my junior year of high school, the answer to all my prayers walked through my history classroom doors on a Wednesday morning. A United States Air Force member visited our class to discuss opportunities for students post high school graduation.

"Who plans on going to college after high school," said the Air Force representative.

Much of the class raised our hands.

"Whose parents have saved at least $50,000 for your college expenses?"

Everyone's hands remained down.

"Who in this room would welcome the opportunity for someone else to pay for all of your college?"

All hands rose again.

"Well," said the Air Force rep, "the United States Air Force has a program just for you. If you qualify, the Air Force will pay for all your college tuition and fees, give you a monthly stipend to live on, as well as provide you with a guaranteed job upon college graduation."

"What's the catch?" I stated as I raised my hand.

"All you have to do is serve four years in the Air Force upon college graduation. After those four years, you're free to get out of the military, or continue for an extended period."

"So, you're saying that the Air Force will pay for all my college, give me money every month, and all I have to do is serve four years in the military after graduation," I responded.

"Yes Sir, you are correct," replied the Air Force rep.

The wheels in my head began to spin in a positive motion. This may be the opportunity I coveted and dreamed of for so long. I was intrigued by the proposition and requested more information from the Air Force rep immediately following his sales pitch to our class. He handed me a brochure and told me to stop by, with my parents, to the Air Force recruiting office anytime to discuss the College Air Force Reserve Officer Training Corps (ROTC) scholarship program. I agreed to discuss this with my parents, and hopefully, I would be seeing him soon.

After school ended that day, I rushed home to tell Larry and my mom the news I had received today. I walked through the front door, finding them both in the kitchen preparing dinner.

"Heyyy!" Mom and Larry shouted as I walked through the door.

"Hey," I said in a short tone to get to the root of my expedited trip home. "I know how I'm going to get my college paid for."

"Really…how," replied my mom.

"Well, the Air Force came to our school today and spoke about their college ROTC program. They said they'll pay for all my college, as long as I serve a four-year commitment immediately after college graduation."

"What else," replied my mom?

"I'll be competitive for a scholarship as long as I'm already accepted to a college, have at least a 24 composite ACT score, pass the Air Force physical fitness test, and have a minimum 3.0 GPA."

"You took your ACT already this year and got above that score and you have a 4.2 GPA. The only thing you have left to do is complete the fitness test and get accepted to college. Are you sure you want to do this?"

"Momma, I don't want any college bills."

"Don't you worry about that. We'll help you with college."

"Momma, you've done enough. I gotta do this. If I can get this scholarship, I won't have to worry about anything but going to school."

"Ok," my mom said enthusiastically. "We'll go down to the recruiter and talk to him this weekend about the details on this."

That Saturday, we went to the Air Force recruiter and he verified that all my information I told my parents was correct. I only had two other requirements to fulfill to become a candidate for the scholarship.

When I went to school on Monday, I set up a fitness test with a counselor for later during the week. I took the test and passed it. My next hurdle was acceptance into the college of my choice.

Initially, I wanted to become an Architect due to the computer aided drafting classes I took with one of my favorite high school teachers, Mr. Nate Moses. I looked at attending the University of Kansas due to them being the first institution to send me information pertaining to attending college.

Architecture was my first love; however, after talking with Mr. Moses, I told him how much I enjoyed working with my hands also. He suggested that maybe I expand my college major search to include engineering. I agreed and conducted a little research as to which engineering discipline I wanted to study.

After reading the engineering descriptions, I concluded that Mechanical Engineering was the right choice for me. I began to research the top Mechanical Engineering schools in the country, and a school near me ranked as one of the top programs in the nation. That school was The University of

Texas at Austin. I told my mom and Larry and we arranged a college tour of the school to see if I would like it.

We attended the tour a couple weeks later and I immediately fell in love with the school. The campus was like a city in itself and it was great. It was exactly what I wanted and needed. Upon returning home, I immediately completed my college application and sent it off, in hopes of my acceptance into The University of Texas at Austin.

In conjunction with submitting my admission application for college, I also submitted my Air Force ROTC scholarship application, with potential selection contingent upon my acceptance into The University of Texas. All I could do now is wait for the results of my college application.

As the weeks passed by, I began to get worried. "Did I fill out the paperwork correctly," I pondered. "Did I not meet the school's requirements," I thought?

I had absolutely no clue of "if" or "when" an acceptance or denial letter would arrive at my house. I waited patiently for over a month before I came home to an unexpected family meeting. I open the door to the house and walk into the living room. My mom and Larry were at the kitchen table, as always; however, this time seemed a little different.

There was a bit of anxiousness in their eyes.

"Everything alright?" I said as I saw their faces.

They said absolutely nothing; however, my mom extended her arm out to me with a white envelope in it. I grabbed it and read the sender's address.

"The University of Texas...Office of Admissions," I read aloud slowly, not comprehending the full extent of what was in my hands.

"Momma...Larry...this is Texas!" My heartbeat was as fast as a drag car on a quarter-mile strip. For as much as I wanted to open the letter, I was a bit scared to.

"Open it!"

"Ok Momma...Ok!" I opened the letter slowly, unfolded the tri-folded piece of paper, and began to read.

"Dear Mr. Nicholas Battle...It is my pleasure to inform you of your acceptance into The University of Texas at Austin. It is also my pleasure to inform you of your acceptance into the Cockrell School of Engineering in pursuant of a degree in Mechanical Engineering!"

"Woooooooooooooooooooo," I yelled! My excitement had overtaken me and I could not contain my emotions. I was truly excited! I looked over at my parents and saw both were a little "misty-eyed," especially my mom. She and I had been through so much. It was me and her against the world for so long.

From the home invasion, to limited household funds, to surviving through some of our darkest times; my mom made sure I was able to make it out of our situation and not become a statistic of our previous environment. She wanted better for me and assured that "better" was what I received. My acceptance to The University of Texas validated everything she lovingly sacrificed for my life. So, when my mom began to shed a few tears after hearing this great news, I understood her joy and relief that the foundation she laid for me resulted in a successful young life thus far.

My excitement was still high from my recent good news; however, my goals were just halfway complete. As ecstatic as I was to learn of my acceptance into college, I was still eager to find out my fate with respect to the Air Force ROTC scholarship program.

To complete the scholarship qualification process, I decided I would bring my college acceptance letter to the Air

Force recruiting office to place it into the final scholarship requirements package. I arrived at the Air Force office the morning following receiving my college acceptance letter. I hand a copy over to the Air Force reps as they include it into my final package. They place a stamp on the package to send it off to the scholarship committee for consideration for a scholarship award. Now, we must begin to wait…again.

A week before Christmas, my waiting would come to an end. I finally received a letter from the United States Air Force. As with my college acceptance letter, I opened it in front of my parents and began to read the letter.

"Memorandum For: Nicholas J. Battle," I began to read. "Congratulations! This memorandum serves official notification of your conditional acceptance in receiving an Air Force ROTC scholarship commencing in the school year 2001-2002. The competition for an Air Force ROTC scholarship involves many of the finest students in the country. Your accomplishment is commendable!"

BATTLE'S BLUEPRINT

Dream it, prepare for it, and 'do' it. Do not be afraid to fail. You can never expect greatness from yourself if you are afraid of disappointment.

After reading the memorandum in its entirety, a great weight lifted off my shoulders. I achieved what I set out to accomplish; to attend college on a full-scholarship to honor the sacrifices my mom made for me. For all that she had done for our family, it was now my time to begin "doing" for her. What better way to "do" this than attending college on a scholarship valued up to $250,000?

These two major accomplishments in my life were a direct reflection on my mother. She instilled in me my work ethic that led to an enduring drive that propelled me to success. She never quit or complained, no matter the cards dealt. Her constant stress of educational excellence propelled me to expect, and not "hope," to be great.

These expectations led me to becoming a member of *Who's Who Amongst American High School Students*, a National Honor Society member, and an 8-time honor roll student; culminating in a final standing of 6 of 660 students in my graduating high school class. Some may say I had truly accomplished all the goals I set for myself; however, this was just the beginning...

THE SOUNDTRACK

(Scan for Apple Soundtrack Playlist)

1. **MAC** – CAN U LOVE ME

2. **NAS** - THE GENESIS

3. **TALIB KWELI** – JOY (FT. MOS DEF)

4. **C-MURDER** - WHERE I'M FROM (FT. PRIME SUSPECTS)

5. **XZIBIT** - THE FOUNDATION

6. **JADAKISS** - WHY? (FT. ANTHONY HAMILTON)

7. **COMPTON'S MOST WANTED** – GROWIN' UP IN THE HOOD

8. **SOULJA SLIM** - U HEAR DAT

9. **U.G.K.** - MURDER

10. **THE NOTORIOUS B.I.G.** - KICK IN THE DOOR

11. **THE GAME** - START FROM SCRATCH

12. **MASTER P** - BACK UP OFF ME

13. **JAY Z** - THIS CAN'T BE LIFE (FT. BEANIE SIGEL & SCARFACE)

14. **THE DIPLOMATS** - I'M READY

15. **NIPSEY HUSSLE** - U DON'T GOT A CLUE

16. **MAC** - FATHER'S DAY

17. **DR. DRE** - LIL' GHETTO BOY (FT. SNOOP DOGG & DAZ)

18. **NAS** - ONE LOVE

19. **KANYE** - REAL FRIENDS (FT. TY$)

20. **THE DOVE SHACK** – SUMMERTIME (IN THE LBC)

21. **METHOD MAN** – YOU'RE ALL I NEED (FT. MARY J BLIGE)

22. **NAS** - SIMPLE THINGS

23. **STYLES P** - BLACK MAGIC (FT. ANGIE STONE)

24. **COMMON** - THE LIGHT

25. **2PAC** - SO MANY TEARS

26. **CORMEGA** - A NEW DAY BEGINS

27. **TEAR DA CLUB UP THUGS** - HYPNOTIZED CASH MONEY (FT. HOT BOYS AND BABY)

28. **T.I.** - DOIN' MY JOB

29. **JAY Z** - WHERE HAVE YOU BEEN (FT. BEANIE SIGEL)

30. **LIL WAYNE** - UP TO ME

31. **WU-TANG** - TRIUMPH

32. **2PAC** - DEAR MAMA

Acknowledgements

This is the most difficult thing to accomplish throughout this writing process because I have so many people to recognize. First off, I must thank God for giving me the strength to complete this book. It took a lot of courage to write this, but He equipped and prepared me to put the pen to paper.

To my wife, my best friend, my rock…Vada, thank you for being the pillar of continuity and stability within our family. You've been here from the beginning and have held me down through everything. Not only are you the wifey, but you're my confidant, soul mate, and outstanding mother to our son…I love you.

To my son, LanLan, you are the absolute best thing that has ever happened to me. Without you, I would have never had the motivation and dedication to write this book. This is for you baby boy. I love you more than words can describe.

Mom…for a long time, it was just you and I. You made me into the man I am today. Without your guidance and strong foundation, you've set for me, I could've lost my way. I am the man I am today because of YOU. For all that you have sacrificed for me, I view some of my greatest accomplishments as seeing you achieve the goals you have set for yourself. When you finished your Bachelor's and Master's degrees, I shed plenty of tears because I knew how challenging it was for you to complete it, but nearly 32 years after your high school graduation, YOU did it! You never gave up on me or yourself. You're the strongest person I know, without a doubt. In the words of the late 2Pac, "There's no way I can pay you back, but my plan is to show you that I understand. You are appreciated." I love you.

Dad, I wouldn't be here without you. A lot of people don't know this, but when I went to college, our relationship flourished big-time. You're my dude…my guy and I love you…no doubt. You've always kept it real with me. You never sugarcoated anything, and I inherited that trait from you…haha. Love you man.

To my beautiful stepmom, Sarah, I've always loved you as if you were my own mother. You treat me as though I am your own. When people ask you how many children you have, you always reply with 3, even though I'm not your biological child. You don't know how much that means to me. You've always been one of my strongest advocates, no matter the situation. I love you so much.

To my sister, Carlena, and brother, Dee…all I ever wanted to do was set the best example a big brother could set for their younger siblings. I hope I've fulfilled in that role. Seeing you 2 accomplish your goals is like seeing my own "children" succeed at life. I know…I know…I'm not your parent, but you 2 know I fuss at y'all like I am…haha. I love you 2 more than the world itself. I just never want to fail you 2.

Larry, you were exactly what I needed in my life when you joined our family. You taught me soooooo much, and I continue to learn from you to this day. You gave me structure…you taught me responsibility. Without you, I honestly don't know where I'd be in life. THANK YOU! I love you.

Grandma and PawPaw, you were my second set of parents. You showed me what a family structure is supposed to look like. PawPaw, you showed me how a man is supposed to act. You were and will always be my hero. Grandma, you made sure I kept my head in the books. You kept me well versed and educated on the topics throughout this world. I only wanted to make you two proud…hopefully I succeeded at that. I miss you both dearly, but I know you're watching over me and my family. My love for you is unconditional.

To my grandmother Vergie, you taught me the importance of work ethic. You showed me what motivation was. You turned an unfortunate situation of having a stroke, into a positive one through your work with the ADA. You traveled across the country, making sure that people with disabilities got the deserved attention they needed in this world and had the opportunity for their issues to be listened to. You never took "no" for an answer. Some of my best memories in life are sitting on your lazy-boy arm chair, sharing a moon pie and blueberry muffin with you. I miss and love you so much.

B.C., you are the older sister I never had. Southern Maid donuts don't taste as good now because I'm not eating them next to you. You taught me, through actions, that family is the most important thing we have in this life, and to this day, you still find a way to herd us all together, even when we think it's impossible. You've never held your tongue for no one, and I appreciate that. I know Aunt Linda is smiling down on you. I love you girl!

John-John and Bryant, forget being uncles, you 2 are like my brothers. Between the 2 of you, I learned so much…how to talk to girls, how to extract every ounce of talent I have out of me…hell, you even taught me how to piss standing up…lol! You 2 don't realize how IRREPLACEABLE you both are in my life, no matter what. You're my brothers for life and I love you.

To my cousin and surrogate brother Jay, we came into this world together, just 13 days apart. We're the sons of 2 brothers and 2 mothers who are best friends to this day. We talk every day, and it's been like that our whole life. You are truly my BROTHER. We think alike, act alike, and most importantly, we respect what each other has to say. I got you and I know you got me...and for that, I love you bro.

Langston and Kash, thank you brothers for writing the foreword section of this book. You guys know me in and out. Kash…my dawg…we've been through so much. From being on tour in Texas, to the countless studio hours in Los Angeles, to starting businesses together…you are truly one of my best friends. Langston, if I have a "twin" in this world that understands me the most, it's you. From day one, we connected through Hip-Hop. I remember the Nas "God's

Son" poster in your dorm room in college…LOL! Since then, I knew we were gonna be rocking like a cut off stocking in the penitentiary trying to get waves (in my inner B.G. voice). I'm honored to call you a friend, and more honored to call you my brother…brother that bleeds blue with me.

Since we're talking about bleeding blue, shout out to my bruhs from the Mighty Mu Rho chapter of Phi Beta Sigma. Lester, Harrison, Jackie, RJ, Reggie, X, Linc, Langston, Antwaun, Jimmy, and Andre (RIP). We brought the "Blue" back to Texas and our cause continues to speed on its way. I love y'all. Bllluuuu Phhhhhhiiiiiii

Additional Titles from the Author

Battle's Blueprint: 5 Self Battles to Defeat for Success

For booking information, visit:

www.NinosCorner.com

About the Author

Nicholas "NinosCorner" Battle is a man of many talents. He's an Air Force veteran, who has deployed to Iraq and Afghanistan in support of Operation Iraqi and Operation Enduring Freedom. Throughout his career, he has managed and executed more than $495 million in government contracts.

Battle is also the Owner and Managing Editor of NinosCorner Sports, where he formulates and tracks metrics to evaluate performance, as well as analyzes and transforms data into strategies for the company and clients. His custom NinosCorner Number (NCN) is utilized by sports agencies to evaluate potential clients.

Under his alias "NinosCorner," Battle is an accomplished music producer with over 50 production credits on his resume. He has produced songs for more than 100 artists and plans to compose a film score in the near future.

Battle received a Master of Science (M.S.) Degree in Technology Intelligence, with a specialization in Cyber and

Data Analytics, from the National Intelligence University, a M.S in Industrial Technology from Texas A&M-Commerce, and a Bachelor of Science (B.S.) degree in Mechanical Engineering from The University of Texas. He also received a Graduate Certificate in Sports Industry Essentials from Columbia University.

When he's not working, his favorite thing to do is watch movies and travel with his family.

To book Nicholas for your next

event, visit: www.NinosCorner.com